The Original
Summer Bridge Activities™

Bridging Grades Second to Third

Caution: Exercise activities may require adult supervision. Before beginning any exercise activity, consult a physician. Written parental permission is suggested for those using this book in group situations. Children should always warm up prior to beginning any exercise activity and should stop immediately if they feel any discomfort during exercise.

Caution: Before beginning any food activity, ask parents' permission and inquire about the child's food allergies and religious or other food restrictions.

Caution: Nature activities may require adult supervision. Before beginning any nature activity, ask parents' permission and inquire about the child's plant and animal allergies. Remind the child not to touch plants or animals during the activity without adult supervision.

Caution: Before completing any balloon activity, ask parents' permission and inquire about possible latex allergies. Also, remember that uninflated or popped balloons may present a choking hazard.

The authors and publisher are not responsible or liable for any injury that may result from performing the exercises or activities in this book.

Credits

Series Creator: Michele D. Van Leeuwen

Content Editor: JulieAnna Kirsch

Copy Editor: Beatrice Allen

Layout and Cover Design: Chasity Rice

Cover Illustration: Robbie Short

Table of Contents

About Summer Learning

Dear Parents:

Did you know that many children experience learning loss when they do not engage in educational activities during the summer? This means that some of what they have spent time learning over the preceding school year evaporates during the summer months. However, summer learning loss is something that you can help prevent. Below are a few suggestions for fun and engaging activities that can help children maintain and grow their academic skills during the summer.

- Read with your child every day. Visit your local library together and select books on subjects that interest your child.

- Ask your child's teacher to recommend books for summer reading.

- Explore parks, nature preserves, museums, and cultural centers.

- Consider every day as a day full of teachable moments. Measuring ingredients for recipes and reviewing maps before a car trip are ways to learn or reinforce skills.

- Each day, set goals for your child to accomplish. For example, complete five math problems or read one section or chapter in a book.

- Encourage your child to complete the activities in books such as Summer Bridge Activities™ to help bridge the summer learning gap.

To learn more about summer learning loss and summer learning programs, visit *www.summerlearning.org.*

Have a memorable summer!

Ron Fairchild

CEO, National Summer Learning Association

About Summer Bridge Activities™

Summer Bridge Activities™: Bridging Grades Second to Third helps prepare your rising third grader for a successful school year. The activities in this book are designed to review the skills that your child mastered in second grade, preview the skills that he or she will learn in third grade, and help prevent summer learning loss. No matter how wonderful your child's classroom experiences are, your involvement outside of the classroom is crucial to his or her academic success. Together with *Summer Bridge Activities™: Bridging Grades Second to Third*, you can fill the summer months with learning experiences that will deepen and enrich your child's knowledge and prepare your child for the upcoming school year.

Summer Bridge Activities™ is the original workbook series developed to help parents support their children academically during the summer months. While many other summer workbook series are available, Summer Bridge Activities™ continues to be the series that teachers recommend most.

The three sections in this workbook correspond to the three months of traditional summer vacation. Each section begins with a goal-setting activity, a word list, and information for parents about the fitness and character development activities located throughout the section.

To achieve maximum results, your child should complete two activity pages each day. Activities cover a range of subjects, including reading, writing, addition and subtraction, grammar, fitness, and character development. These age-appropriate activities are presented in a fun and creative way to challenge and engage your child. Each activity page is numbered by day, and each day includes a space for your child to place a colorful, motivational sticker after he or she completes the day's activities.

Bonus extension activities that encourage outdoor learning, science experiments, and social studies exercises are located at the end of each section. Complete these activities with your child throughout each month as time allows.

An answer key located at the end of the book allows you to check your child's work. The included flash cards help reinforce basic skills, and a certificate of completion will help you and your child celebrate his or her summer learning success!

Skills Matrix

Day	Addition	Algebra	Character Development	Division	Fitness	Fractions	Geometry & Measurement	Grammar	Graphing & Probability	Language Arts	Multiplication	Number Sense	Phonics	Problem Solving	Reading Comprehension	Science	Social Studies	Subtraction	Time & Money	Vocabulary & Spelling	Writing
1								★		★		★	★								
2					★			★		★		★									
3								★				★			★						
4								★				★	★							★	
5								★				★	★							★	
6								★				★			★						
7								★				★								★	★
8	★							★		★		★						★			
9	★							★		★		★						★			
10	★		★					★		★								★			
11								★				★	★							★	
12	★							★		★		★									
13	★							★							★						
14								★		★								★			★
15					★			★				★			★						
16								★						★	★						
17	★							★					★		★			★			
18	★							★		★		★									
19								★				★			★			★			
20	★							★		★								★			★
								★		★	BONUS PAGES!					★	★			★	
1	★							★				★								★	
2								★							★			★			
3	★				★			★										★		★	
4	★							★								★				★	
5	★							★							★			★			
6								★		★									★		★
7										★							★		★	★	
8								★							★				★		
9			★					★		★									★		
10										★									★	★	
11								★							★				★		

Skills Matrix

Day	Addition	Algebra	Character Development	Division	Fitness	Fractions	Geometry & Measurement	Grammar	Graphing & Probability	Language Arts	Multiplication	Number Sense	Phonics	Problem Solving	Reading Comprehension	Science	Social Studies	Subtraction	Time & Money	Vocabulary & Spelling	Writing
12								★		★									★		★
13	★				★			★							★			★			
14							★	★							★						
15							★	★		★					★						
16							★	★		★										★	
17							★	★							★						
18							★	★							★					★	
19								★		★											★
20							★	★							★						
BONUS PAGES!							★	★								★	★				
1							★	★		★					★						
2							★	★		★											★
3	★							★							★			★			
4					★		★	★		★											
5							★	★		★					★						
6								★			★				★						
7								★		★	★										
8								★			★				★						★
9				★				★		★					★						
10				★				★		★											
11				★				★		★						★					
12		★						★							★						
13		★	★					★							★						
14						★		★		★											
15						★		★							★						
16						★	★	★		★											
17						★		★	★	★											
18								★	★						★					★	
19								★	★						★						★
20								★	★						★						
BONUS PAGES!	★		★													★	★	★			

Encouraging Summer Reading

Literacy is the single most important skill that your child needs to be successful in school. The following list includes ideas of ways that you can help your child discover the great adventures of reading!

- Establish a time for reading each day. Ask your child about what he or she is reading. Try to relate the material to an event that is happening this summer or to another book or story.

- Let your child see you reading for enjoyment. Talk about the great things that you discover when you read.

- Create a summer reading list. Choose books from the reading list (pages ix–x) or head to the library and explore the shelves. A general rule for selecting books at the appropriate reading level is to choose a page and ask your child to read it aloud. If he or she does not know more than five words on the page, the book may be too difficult.

- Read newspaper and magazine articles, recipes, menus, maps, and street signs on a daily basis to show your child the importance of reading.

- Find books that relate to your child's experiences. For example, if you are going camping, find a book about camping. This will help your child develop new interests.

- Visit the library each week. Let your child choose his or her own books, but do not hesitate to ask your librarian for suggestions. Often, librarians can recommend books based on what your child enjoyed in the past.

- Make up stories. This is especially fun to do in the car, on camping trips, or while waiting at the airport. Encourage your child to tell a story with a beginning, a middle, and an end. Or, have your child start a story and let other family members build on it.

- Encourage your child to join a summer reading club at the library or a local bookstore. Your child may enjoy talking to other children about the books that he or she has read.

Summer Reading List

The summer reading list includes fiction and nonfiction titles. Experts recommend that second- and third-grade students read for at least 20 minutes each day. Then, ask questions about the story to reinforce comprehension.

Decide on an amount of daily reading time for each month. You may want to write the time on each Monthly Goals page at the beginning of each section.

Fiction

Blume, Judy
The Pain and the Great One

Bunting, Eve
So Far from the Sea

Burns, Marilyn
Spaghetti and Meatballs for All!

Chbosky, Stacy
Who Owns the Sun?

Cherry, Lynne
The Great Kapok Tree: A Tale of the Amazon Rain Forest

Cleary, Beverly
Ramona the Pest

Curtis, Gavin
The Bat Boy and His Violin

DeGross, Monalisa
Donovan's Word Jar

dePaola, Tomie
The Art Lesson

Estes, Eleanor
The Hundred Dresses

Falwell, Cathryn
Word Wizard

Hopkinson, Deborah
Sweet Clara and the Freedom Quilt

Keats, Ezra Jack
Peter's Chair

MacLachlan, Patricia
All the Places to Love

Palatini, Margie
Bedhead
Sweet Tooth

Parish, Peggy
Amelia Bedelia

Pilkey, Dav
Dog Breath

Polacco, Patricia
Thunder Cake

Rylant, Cynthia
An Angel for Solomon Singer

Say, Allen
Grandfather's Journey

Schotter, Roni
Nothing Ever Happens on 90th Street

Scieszka, Jon
Math Curse
The True Story of the Three Little Pigs

Summer Reading List (continued)

Fiction (continued)

Seuss, Dr.
The Lorax

Shasha, Mark
Night of the Moonjellies

Silverstein, Shel
A Light in the Attic

Steig, William
Brave Irene

Storad, Conrad J.
Lizards for Lunch: A Roadrunner's Tale

Titus, Eve
Basil of Baker Street

Uchida, Yoshiko
The Bracelet

Van Allsburg, Chris
The Polar Express

Waber, Bernard
Lyle, Lyle, Crocodile

Williams, Margery
The Velveteen Rabbit

Wisniewski, David
The Secret Knowledge of Grown-Ups

Nonfiction

Anno, Masaichiro and Mitsumasa
Anno's Mysterious Multiplying Jar

Carle, Eric
The Tiny Seed

Christian, Peggy
If You Find a Rock

Dobson, David
Can We Save Them? Endangered Species of North America

DK Publishing
Eye Wonder: Mammals
Eye Wonder: Invention

George, Jean Craighead
The Tarantula in My Purse and 172 Other Wild Pets

Gibbons, Gail
Nature's Green Umbrella

Goldish, Meish
Does the Moon Change Shape?

Lester, Helen
Author: A True Story

Locker, Thomas
Water Dance

Schwartz, David M.
How Much Is a Million?

Walker, Sarah
Eye Wonder: Dinosaur

Monthly Goals

A *goal* is something that you want to accomplish. Sometimes, reaching a goal can be hard work!

Think of three goals to set for yourself this month. For example, you may want to read for 30 minutes each day. Write your goals on the lines and review them with an adult.

Place a sticker next to each goal that you complete. Feel proud that you have met your goals!

1. _____ PLACE STICKER HERE

2. _____ PLACE STICKER HERE

3. _____ PLACE STICKER HERE

Word List

The following words are used in this section. They are good words for you to know. Read each word. Use a dictionary to look up each word that you do not know. Then, write two sentences. Use a word from the word list in each sentence.

coast	glide
crops	history
flexible	shadow
gentle	tame
germs	vapor

1. _____

_____

2. _____

_____

Introduction to Flexibility

This section includes fitness and character development activities that focus on flexibility. These activities are designed to get you moving and thinking about building your physical fitness and your character.

Physical Flexibility

For many people, being flexible means easily doing everyday tasks, such as bending to tie a shoe. Tasks like this can be hard for people who do not stretch often.

Stretching will make your muscles more flexible. It can also improve your balance and coordination.

You probably stretch every day without realizing it. Do you ever reach for a dropped pencil or a box of cereal on the top shelf? If you do, then you are stretching. Try to improve your flexibility this summer. Set a stretching goal. For example, you might stretch every day until you can touch your toes.

Flexibility of Character

It is good to have a flexible body. It is also good to be mentally flexible. This means being open to change.

It can be upsetting when things do not go your way. Can you think of a time when an unexpected event ruined your plans? For example, a family trip to the zoo was canceled because the car had a flat tire.

Unexpected events happen sometimes. How you react to those events often affects the outcome. Arm yourself with the tools to be flexible. Have realistic expectations. Find ways to make the situation better. Look for good things that may have come from the event.

You can be mentally flexible by showing respect to other people. Sharing and taking turns are also ways to be mentally flexible. This character trait gets easier with practice. Over the summer, practice and use your mental flexibility often.

Circle the correct numeral for each number word.

1. forty-five

   54 (45)

2. fifty-eight

   (58) 85

3. eighty-one

   18 (81)

4. thirty

   (30) 31

5. three

   30 (3)

6. fifteen

   (15) 50

Write the number word for each numeral.

0: *zero*   20: *twenty*   30: *thirty*

40: *forty*   60: *sixty*   80: *eighty*

A noun is a person, place, or thing. Write each noun from the word bank in the correct column.

| aunt ✓ | city ✓ | cloud ✓ | desert ✓ | friend ✓ | gym ✓ |
| letter ✓ | officer ✓ | plate ✓ | prince ✓ | shoe ✓ | store ✓ |

Person	Place	Thing
aunt	city	letter
officer	gym	cloud
prince	store	plate
friend		shoe
		desert

DAY 1

Read each word aloud. Write the number of syllables you hear. Then, write the number of vowel sounds you hear.

Word	Syllables	Vowel Sounds
EXAMPLE: rabbit	2	2
7. three	1	21
8. red	1	1
9. window	2	2
10. elephant	3	3

Word	Syllables	Vowel Sounds
11. playful	2	2
12. lady	2	2
13. favorite	2	4
14. nine	1	2
15. truck	1	1

Read each word in the word bank. Write the soft c words under the celery. Write the hard c words under the carrot.

cake ✓   coat ✓   cell ✓   city ✓
century ✓   cat ✓   cave ✓   cent ✓

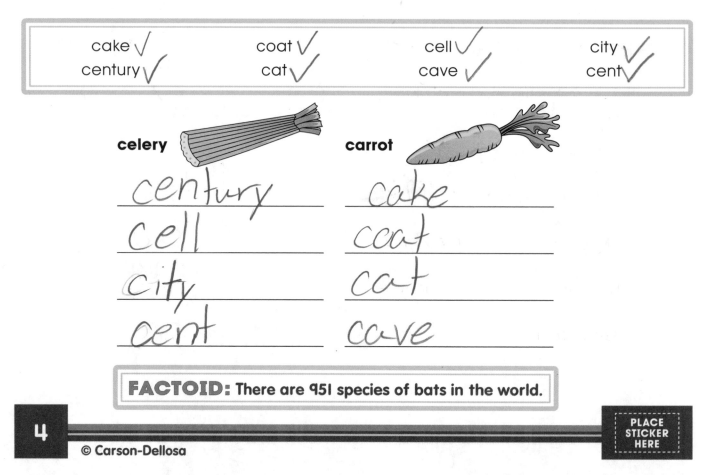

celery

century
cell
city
cent

carrot

cake
coat
cat
cave

FACTOID: There are 951 species of bats in the world.

PLACE STICKER HERE

A cardinal number tells *how many* or *how much* and can be written as a numeral (80) or as a number word (eighty). An ordinal number tells the position of an item in a series (eightieth). Fill in the chart with the cardinal numbers, ordinal number words, or ordinal numerals.

	Cardinal Number	Ordinal Number Word	Ordinal Numeral
1.	20	*twenty*	*twentieth*
2.	*60*	sixty	*sixtieth*
3.	*36*	thirty-six	*thirty-sixth*
4.	77	*seventy-seven*	*seventy-seventh*
5.	*5*	*five*	fifth

Circle the nouns in each sentence. The number in parentheses tells how many nouns are in each sentence.

6. The (boy) found a pink and white (shell) at the (beach). (3)

7. My (aunt) owns a (store) in the (country). (3)

8. The (cloud) is shaped like a (rabbit). (2)

9. The (letter) is from my (friend). (2)

10. The (girl) put the (glass) in the (kitchen). (3)

11. The (kite) sailed with the (breeze). (2)

12. (Anna) read a (book) about (manatees). (3)

13. (Owen) and (Cass) hiked past the (cave). (3)

DAY 2

Draw lines to connect syllables to form complete words.

14. pen   met
      sun   cil
      hel   on
      drag   dae

15. blos   som
      rab   der
      spi   bit
      ti   ger

16. car   en
      pup   rot
      can   py
      sev   dy

17. won   ry
      sum   der
      crick   mer
      mar   et

18. can   cus
      pen   fin
      muf   dle
      cir   cil

19. pea   dow
      dol   lar
      mit   ten
      win   nut

Stand and Stretch

Test your flexibility with this stretching challenge. Remember to stretch slowly. It takes practice to improve flexibility.

Stand tall and hold a ruler in one hand. Bend slowly at the waist. Reach down until the tip of the ruler touches the ground. Check the ruler to find how close you are to touching the ground. If you can already touch the ground, try to flatten your hands to the floor. Stretch three times. Record your best measurement. Complete this test each week and compare your results.

FITNESS FLASH: Practice a V-sit. Stretch five times.

* See page ii.

PLACE
STICKER
HERE

Write the number that comes before, between, or after each number or numbers.

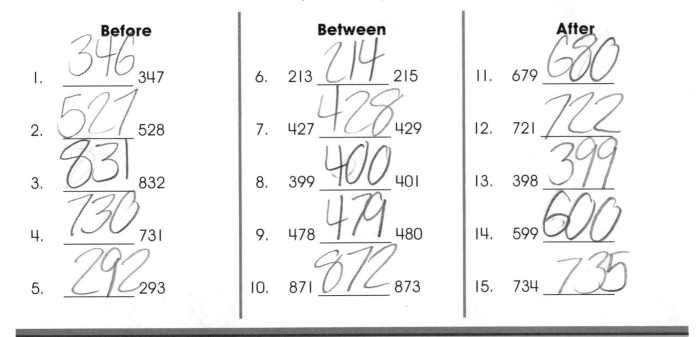

	Before		Between		After
1.	_346_ 347	6. 213 _214_ 215	11. 679 _680_
2.	_527_ 528	7. 427 _428_ 429	12. 721 _722_
3.	_831_ 832	8. 399 _400_ 401	13. 398 _399_
4.	_730_ 731	9. 478 _479_ 480	14. 599 _600_
5.	_292_ 293	10. 871 _872_ 873	15. 734 _735_

Write _person_, _place_, or _thing_ to identify each underlined noun.

16. The <u>child</u> ate lunch at noon. _person_

17. They went to the <u>park</u> to play soccer. _place_

18. The <u>teacher</u> heard the children sing. _person_

19. The boys and girls rowed a <u>boat</u>. _thing_

20. One girl went down the <u>slide</u>. _thing_

21. Kendra and her dad went to the <u>store</u>. _place_

22. <u>Winston</u> planted the pumpkin seeds. _person_

23. Nadia's missing <u>shoe</u> was under the sofa. _thing_

Read the passage. Then, answer the questions.

Helpful Insects and Arachnids

Some insects can destroy crops, such as fruits and vegetables, by eating them. Not all insects are bad, though. Some insects help people. Bees move pollen from flower to flower. This helps flowers make seeds so that there will be more flowers the next year. Bees also produce honey. Ladybugs are helpful insects too. They eat the insects that chew on plants. Finally, spiders may look scary, but they are helpful. They are not insects. They are arachnids. They catch flies, crickets, and moths in their webs. If you find a spider in your home, ask an adult to help you carefully place it outside. Then, it can do its job.

24. What is the main idea of this passage?

 A. Insects can destroy crops.

 B. Ladybugs are beautiful.

 C. Some insects and arachnids are helpful.

25. What do bees produce? _Honey_

26. How do bees help flowers grow? _They move pollen from flower to flower._

27. How are ladybugs helpful? _They eat insects that chew on plants._

28. What do spiders catch in their webs? _Flies, crickets, and moths._

FACTOID: Ladybugs chew their food from side to side, not up and down.

© Carson-Dellosa

PLACE STICKER HERE

Write > (greater than) or < (less than) to compare each pair of numbers.

1. 2 $<$ 4

2. 64 $>$ 46

3. 322 $>$ 100

4. 19 $<$ 91

5. 29 $<$ 30

6. 985 $>$ 850

7. 14 $>$ 4

8. 124 $<$ 216

9. 648 $<$ 846

10. 9 $<$ 10

11. 592 $>$ 324

12. 745 $<$ 746

Write a noun from the word bank to complete each sentence.

| bank ✓ | bike ✓ | camera ✓ | hero ✓ | mud ✓ | palace ✓ |

13. The rain turned the dirt into ___mud___.

14. I took a picture of my family with a ___camera___.

15. The tires on the ___bike___ needed air.

16. I put the money I saved in a ___bank___.

17. The ___hero___ of the story was a man who helped people.

18. The king and queen live in a ___palace___.

Synonyms are words that have the same meaning. Read the story. Then, write a synonym from the word bank for each underlined word.

| happy ✓ | outdoors ✓ | notice ✓ | run ✓ | trail ✓ | woods ✓ |

Jogging with Mom

Mom and I like to jog every evening. We sometimes take our dog, Rudy. We turn down a path and jog through the forest. We see the tall trees and listen to our feet hitting the ground. Being outside at sundown makes me feel joyful.

19. jog _run_
20. path _trail_
21. forest _woods_
22. see _notice_
23. outside _outdoors_
24. joyful _happy_

Read each word aloud. Listen to the vowel sounds. If the word has a short vowel sound, write **S** on the line. If the word has a long vowel sound, write **L** on the line.
EXAMPLE:

just **S**

25. cape _L_
26. clock _S_
27. cute _L_
28. bug _S_
29. ship _S_
30. nice _L_
31. apple _S_
32. goat _L_
33. road _L_
34. help _S_
35. read _L_

FITNESS FLASH: Touch your toes 10 times.

* See page ii.

Find the place value of each underlined digit. Circle the answer.

EXAMPLE:

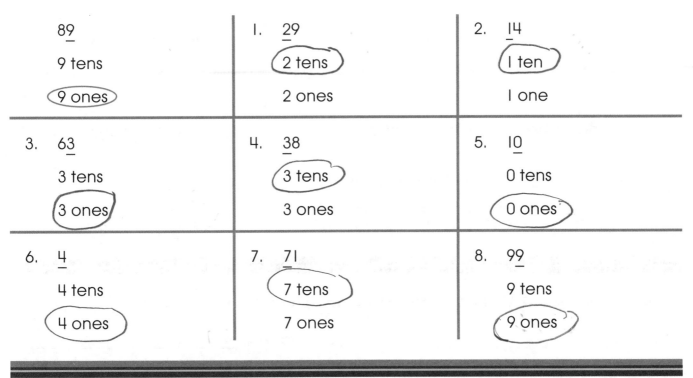

89

9 tens

(9 ones)

1. 29

    (2 tens)

    2 ones

2. 14

    (1 ten)

    1 one

3. 63

    3 tens

    (3 ones)

4. 38

    (3 tens)

    3 ones

5. 10

    0 tens

    (0 ones)

6. 4

    4 tens

    (4 ones)

7. 71

    (7 tens)

    7 ones

8. 99

    9 tens

    (9 ones)

A proper noun names a specific person, place, or thing. Each word of a proper noun begins with a capital letter. Write the name of each person correctly.

9. cindy lewis _Cindy Lewis_

10. nicholas jones _Nicholas Jones_

11. ms. cohen _Ms. Cohen_

12. don li _Don Li_

13. mr. finley _Mr. Finley_

14. ellen garza _Ellen Garza_

15. dr. monica seth _Dr. Monica Seth_

DAY 5

Antonyms are words that have opposite meanings. Read each sentence. Then, circle the antonym for the underlined word in each sentence.

16. Praise your friends when they do <u>good</u> work. （bad） funny

17. Mom told me to wear <u>clean</u> clothes. （dirty） new

18. We should be <u>quiet</u> at the playground. soft （noisy）

19. The bread I <u>bought</u> last week was old. （sold） found

20. I rode my <u>new</u> scooter to Hannah's house. （old） green

Read each word aloud. Then, write *short* or *long* for each vowel sound.

21. bug *short*
22. cake *long*
23. cut *short*
24. gum *short*
25. road *short*
26. catch *short*
27. cube *long*
28. clock *short*
29. stick *short*
30. child *long*
31. mop *short*
32. these *long*
33. street *long*
34. log *short*
35. fly *long*
36. boat *short*

CHARACTER CHECK: Think of a book or movie character who shows kindness. How does the character show kindness?

PLACE STICKER HERE

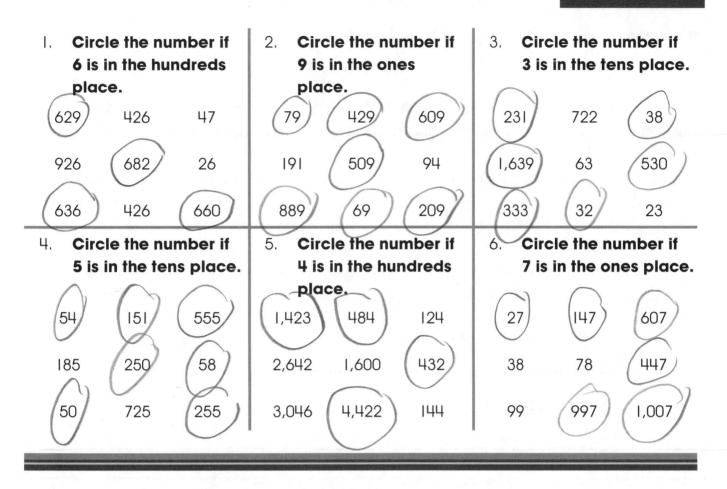

1. **Circle the number if 6 is in the hundreds place.**

(629)   426   47

926   (682)   26

(636)   426   (660)

2. **Circle the number if 9 is in the ones place.**

79   (429)   609

191   (509)   94

889   (69)   (209)

3. **Circle the number if 3 is in the tens place.**

(231)   722   (38)

(1,639)   63   (530)

(333)   (32)   23

4. **Circle the number if 5 is in the tens place.**

(54)   (151)   (555)

185   (250)   (58)

(50)   725   (255)

5. **Circle the number if 4 is in the hundreds place.**

(1,423)   (484)   124

2,642   1,600   (432)

(3,046)   (4,422)   144

6. **Circle the number if 7 is in the ones place.**

(27)   (147)   (607)

38   78   (447)

99   (997)   (1,007)

Underline the proper noun in each sentence.

7. Do you like to visit <u>Jefferson Library</u>?

8. <u>Woodland School</u> is where he will go to school next year.

9. My grandmother lives in <u>France</u>.

10. <u>Roberto's</u> is my favorite restaurant.

11. My cat <u>Fifi</u> likes to sleep all day.

12. <u>Julia</u> is my best friend.

13. <u>Renee</u> shares a computer with her brother.

DAY 6

Read the passage. Then, answer the questions.

Railroads

Railroads have played an important part in history. For centuries, railroads have helped carry people and goods long distances. In the United States, travel was much harder before a railroad connected the eastern and western parts of the country. Workers in the eastern United States built a railroad heading west. A different crew in the west started building a railroad heading east. In 1869, the two lines met in the state of Utah. The crews hammered in a special golden nail to tie the two tracks together. After that, people could travel easily and quickly from one coast of the United States to the other! The next time you stop at a railroad crossing to let a train pass, think about how important railroads have been in history.

14. What is the main idea of this passage?

    A. Railroads played an important part in history.

    B. No one uses railroads today.

    C. You have to stop to let trains go by.

15. What could people do once the railroad was completed? _travel_
    easily and quickly

16. Where did the two railroads begin? _Utah_

17. What did the crews use to join the two tracks? _a special_
    golden nail

FACTOID: A shark can grow a new tooth in 24 hours.

© Carson-Dellosa

Read and answer each question.
EXAMPLE:

Circle the digits that are in the tens place.

2,4②1 3②8 ⑥1

5③6 ⑧4 1,6⓪2

1. Circle the digits that are in the thousands place.

⑦,816 121 ⑥,211

44 729 ④,864

2. Circle the digits that are in the ones place.

2⑥ 84② 46③

92④ 1⑨ 84⑥

3. Circle the digits that are in the hundreds place.

④81 ⑥43 ⑨70

1,②94 1,①22 2,③51

4. What does the circled number mean? 51⑥

(6 ones) 6 tens 6 hundreds

5. What does the circled number mean? ②64

2 ones 2 tens (2 hundreds)

Write each noun and proper noun from the word bank in the correct column.

April ✓   farmer ✓   man ✓   Mexico City ✓   Ms. Sho ✓
park ✓   Sunny Market ✓   teacher ✓   Thursday ✓   ticket ✓

Noun	**Proper Noun**
park	April
farmer	Sunny Market
man	Mexico City
teacher	Thursday
ticket	Ms. Sho

DAY 7

Homophones are words that sound the same but are spelled differently and have different meanings. Write a homophone from the word bank for each underlined word.

bee	new	one	right	wood

6. Did you <u>write</u> the _right_ answer?

7. Nathan only <u>won</u> _one_ game.

8. <u>Would</u> you cut some _wood_ for the fireplace?

9. <u>Be</u> careful, or that _bee_ will sting you!

10. I <u>knew</u> I would get some _new_ shoes.

Think about your favorite holiday. Describe this holiday using each of your five senses. What do you see, hear, feel, smell, and taste?

My favorite day is Christmas.
I see lights, I hear bells,
I feel a Christmas tree.
I smell food. I taste turkey.

FITNESS FLASH: Do arm circles for 30 seconds.

* See page ii.

PLACE STICKER HERE

Add or subtract to solve each problem.

1. 7
    + 2
    9

2. 0
    + 3
    3

3. 8
    + 3
    11

4. 6
    + 2
    8

5. 9
    + 0
    9

6. 3
    − 2
    1

7. 5
    − 0
    5

8. 5
    − 2
    3

9. 10
    − 2
    8

10. 7
    − 3
    4

11. 5
    − 3
    2

12. 6
    + 4
    10

13. 7
    − 2
    5

14. 8
    − 4
    4

15. 2
    + 2
    4

Write each singular or plural noun from the word bank in the correct column.

| fork ✓ | crickets ✓ | guitar ✓ | keys ✓ |
| peanut ✓ | pond ✓ | shirts ✓ | toes ✓ |

Singular	**Plural**
fork	crickets
peanut	shirts
pond	keys
guitar	toes

DAY 8

When a prefix is added to a base word, it changes the meaning of the word. Circle the prefix in each word. Then, write the letter of the correct definition next to the word.

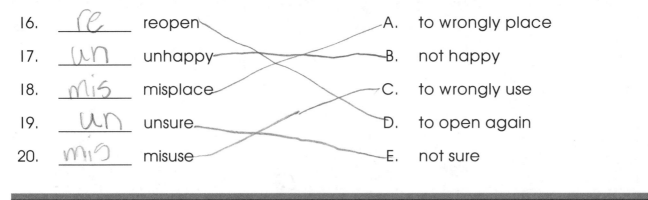

16. _re_ reopen   A. to wrongly place

17. _un_ unhappy   B. not happy

18. _mis_ misplace   C. to wrongly use

19. _un_ unsure   D. to open again

20. _mis_ misuse   E. not sure

Look at each word. Write how many vowels you see. Then, read each word aloud. Write how many vowel sounds you hear.

		Vowels	Vowel Sounds				Vowels	Vowel Sounds
21.	puzzle	2	1		29.	radio	3	3
22.	cookies	4	3		30.	carrot	2	2
23.	blocks	1	1		31.	sleep	2	2
24.	alphabet	3	3		32.	wanted	2	2
25.	goat	2	1		33.	heart	2	1
26.	jump	1	1		34.	useful	2	1
27.	pilot	2	2		35.	beautiful	5	4
28.	lion	2	2		36.	water	2	2

FACTOID: Frogs can jump more than 10 times their own body length.

PLACE STICKER HERE

Write the related facts for each fact family.

1.

II
6 5

$6 + 5 = 11$
$5 + 6 = 11$
$11 - 6 = 5$
$11 - 5 = 6$

2.

4
5 9

$4 + 5 = 9$
$5 + 4 = 9$
$9 - 5 = 4$
$9 - 4 = 5$

3.

7
5 12

$7 + 5 = 12$
$5 + 7 = 12$
$12 - 7 = 5$
$12 - 5 = 7$

Circle the correct word to complete each sentence.

4. · Mark planted a (tree, trees) in his backyard.

5. Sam and his mother bought two (apple, apples) at the grocery store.

6. Andrea fed each dog one (treat, treats).

7. There were three (flag, flags) at the store.

8. All of the (swing, swings) in the park were full.

9. Talia has a new (sister, sisters).

10. I like to draw (picture, pictures).

DAY 9

When a suffix is added to a base word, it changes the meaning of the word. Add -less or -ness to the base word in each sentence.
EXAMPLE:

The children were very ___rest**less**___ today.

11. The ___friendli nes___ of the people made us feel at home.

12. Trying to train my dog to roll over is ___hope less___.

13. The baby loves the ___soft ness___ of her blanket.

14. The ___loud ness___ of the noise made me jump.

15. Her ___happi ness___ showed on her face.

Read each word in the word bank. If the y makes the long i sound, as in *fly*, write the word under the fly. If the y makes the long e sound, as in *baby*, write the word under the baby.

| city | dry | eye | happy | sky | story |

fly

dry
eye
sky

baby

city
happy
story

FITNESS FLASH: Do 10 shoulder shrugs.

* See page ii.

PLACE STICKER HERE

20

Write the missing sign (+, –, or =) in each number sentence.

1. 6 __+__ 3 = 9

2. 12 __–__ 6 = 6

3. 4 __+__ 2 = 2

4. 4 + 3 __=__ 7

5. 14 __+__ 1 = 15

6. 12 __–__ 2 = 10

7. 9 __–__ 3 = 6

8. 14 __+__ 4 = 10

9. 14 – 7 __=__ 7

10. 4 __+__ 1 = 3

11. 7 – 3 __–__ 4

12. 3 __+__ 3 = 6

13. 8 __+__ 4 = 12

14. 9 __+__ 2 = 11

15. 11 __–__ 2 = 9

Circle the word that completes each sentence.

16. Two _____ went for a ride.   girl   (girls)

17. My _____ broke when it fell.   (dish)   dishes

18. Which _____ is yours?   (pencil)   pencils

19. Put all of the _____ back on the shelf.   book   (books)

20. My foot is nine _____ long.   inch   (inches)

21. How many _____ were in the race?   boat   (boats)

22. May I have a piece of _____ ?   (pie)   pies

23. Where are my _____ ?   shoe   (shoes)

24. That _____ belongs to Roger.   (paper)   papers

25. Angelica made a _____ for Sarah.   (gift)   gifts

DAY 10

Underline the compound word in each sentence. Then, draw a line between the two word parts.
EXAMPLE:

Rebecca lives on a <u>house|boat</u>.

26. A rain|drop hit the white rabbit on the nose.

27. Let's go visit the light|house.

28. Did you hear the door|bell ring?

29. The horses are in the barn|yard.

30. I cleaned my bed|room this morning.

31. The snow|flakes fell very quickly.

Fairness First

Everyone wants to be treated fairly. Being fair means treating others like you want to be treated. Think about a time when you were treated unfairly. How did that make you feel? Read the following situations. On another sheet of paper, write about what you would do in each situation.

- You have two friends who are staying at your house after your party. It is time for a snack, and you each want a leftover cupcake. Only two cupcakes are left. What would you do?

- Your younger sister is learning to play a new board game. She asks you to play it with her. As you play, you see that she gave you an extra card. The card will help you win. What would you do?

> **CHARACTER CHECK:** Help a friend or family member with a task today, such as folding laundry or taking out the trash.

PLACE STICKER HERE

Solve each problem.

1. Allison had 8 baseballs. She lost 2 of them. How many baseballs does she have left?

    6

2. Liam had 6 apples. He gave 4 apples away. How many apples does Liam have left?

    2

3. Shannon walked 2 miles. Lori walked 3 miles. How many total miles did the children walk?

    5

4. Nassim saw 8 puppies. Joy saw 4 puppies. How many total puppies did the children see?

    12

Solve each riddle. Write the correct singular and plural forms.

5. I am made of paper, and I have a cover. My name rhymes with <u>look</u>.

    I am a ___book___ . My plural form is ___books___ .

6. I am a round, fuzzy, and sweet fruit. My name rhymes with *beach*.

    I am a ___peach___ . My plural form is ___peaches___ .

7. I can be made of sticks and grass, and birds live in me.

    I am a ___nest___ . My plural form is ___nests___ .

DAY 11

Read each sentence. Then, write the letter of the underlined word's definition.
EXAMPLE:

_____**B**_____ The birds can <u>fly</u>.   A.   a small winged insect

_____**A**_____ The spider ate the <u>fly</u>.   B.   to move through the air

---

8. _____A_____ Please turn on the <u>light</u>.   A.   a lamp

   _____B_____ The box is <u>light</u>.   B.   not heavy

---

9. _____B_____ <u>Store</u> the books on the shelf.   A.   a place to buy things

   _____A_____ I bought a dress at the <u>store</u>. B.   to put away for the future

---

10. _____B_____ Drop a penny in the <u>well</u>.   A.   healthy

    _____A_____ Are you feeling <u>well</u>?   B.   a hole to access underground

                                                          water

Circle each word that has the /o͞o/ sound, as in *tooth*. Draw an X on each word that has the /o͝o/ sound, as in *hook*.

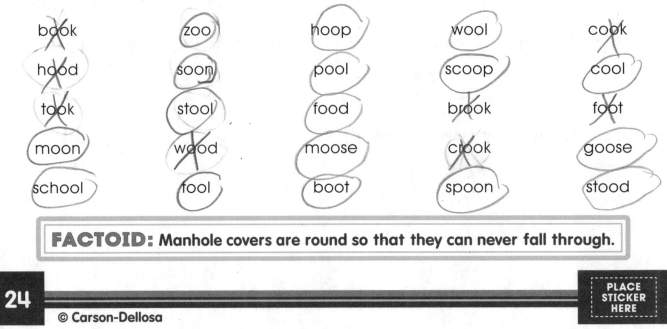

book   zoo   hoop   wool   cook
hood   soon   pool   scoop   cool
took   stool   food   brook   foot
moon   wood   moose   crook   goose
school fool   boot   spoon   stood

> **FACTOID:** Manhole covers are round so that they can never fall through.

PLACE
STICKER
HERE

Draw a line to match the problems that have the same sum.
EXAMPLE:

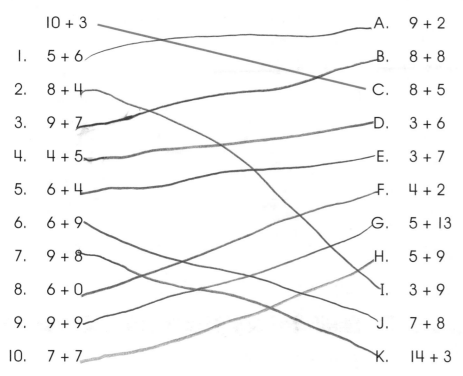

	10 + 3	A.	9 + 2
1.	5 + 6	B.	8 + 8
2.	8 + 4	C.	8 + 5
3.	9 + 7	D.	3 + 6
4.	4 + 5	E.	3 + 7
5.	6 + 4	F.	4 + 2
6.	6 + 9	G.	5 + 13
7.	9 + 8	H.	5 + 9
8.	6 + 0	I.	3 + 9
9.	9 + 9	J.	7 + 8
10.	7 + 7	K.	14 + 3

Change the spelling of each underlined word to make it plural. Use the word bank if you need help.

word bank
feet
geese
knives
leaves
men
mice
teeth

11. more than one <u>man</u> _men_

12. more than one <u>tooth</u> _teeth_

13. more than one <u>leaf</u> _leaves_

14. more than one <u>goose</u> _geese_

15. more than one <u>knife</u> _knifes_

16. more than one <u>mouse</u> _mice_

17. more than one <u>foot</u> _feet_

DAY 12

Write each word from the word bank under the correct heading.

shirt ✓   pliers ✓   socks ✓   screwdriver ✓   elephant ✓   bear ✓
saw ✓   pants ✓   hammer ✓   fox ✓   deer ✓   hat ✓

Animals	Tools	Clothing
fox	saw	shirt
deer	pliers	pants
elephant	hammer	socks
bear	screwdriver	hat

Write *str-*, *spr-*, *spl-*, or *thr-* to complete each word.

18. str eet

19. str ough

20. str ang

21. spl ash

22. spl it

23. thr ow

24. spr ong

25. thr ee

26. str ay

27. spl atter

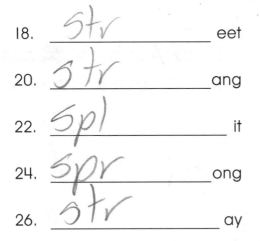

FITNESS FLASH: Practice a V-sit. Stretch five times.

* See page ii.

PLACE STICKER HERE

Add to find each sum.

1. 2
   3
   + 2
   7

2. 4
   4
   + 2
   10

3. 5
   1
   + 1
   7

4. 9
   1
   + 0
   10

5. 7
   2
   + 1
   10

6. 1
   2
   + 6
   9

7. 5
   2
   + 5
   12

8. 6
   1
   + 7
   13

9. 2
   5
   + 4
   11

10. 8
    1
    + 2
    11

11. 2 + 2 + 2 = **6**

12. 0 + 0 + 8 = **8**

13. 1 + 0 + 8 = **9**

14. 5 + 1 + 1 = **7**

15. 2 + 5 + 3 = **10**

16. 9 + 2 + 2 = **13**

Write he, she, it, or they in place of the underlined word or words.

17. The computer was a gift to the school.

    It was a gift to the school.

18. The Johnsons moved into the house next door.

    They moved into the house next door.

19. Dad likes to cook on the weekends.

    He likes to cook on the weekends.

20. Clara Barton was a nurse.

    She was a nurse.

DAY 13

Read the passage. Then, answer the questions.

Washing Your Hands

Your family and teachers have probably told you many times to wash your hands. You should use warm water and soap. Rub your hands together for as long as it takes to sing the alphabet. Then, sing the song again while you rinse your hands. Soap washes off the **germs**, which are tiny cells that can make you sick. If you do not wash your hands, you can pass a sickness to a friend. Also, you could spread the germs to your eyes or mouth if you touch them before washing your hands. Always remember to wash your hands!

21. What is the main idea of this passage?

    A. Cells can make you sick.

    B. Rub your hands together.

    C. You should wash your hands.

22. How long should you rub your hands together? _As long as it takes to sing the alphabet._

23. What does soap do? _Wash off the germs._

24. What does the word *germs* mean?

    A. kinds of soap

    B. tiny cells that can make you sick

    C. ways to wash your hands

25. What could happen if you do not wash your hands? _You could pass a sickness. Or spread germs to your eyes or mouth._

FACTOID: No word in the English language rhymes with film, gulf, or wolf.

PLACE STICKER HERE

Subtract to find each difference.

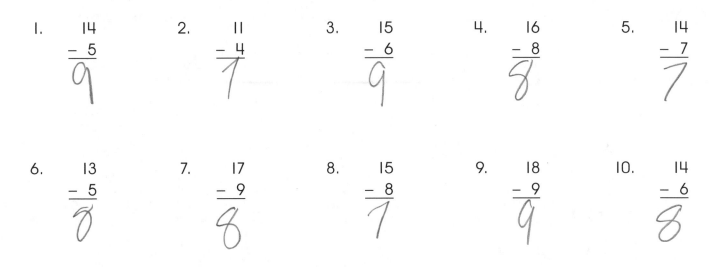

1.
$$14$$
$$- 5$$
9

2.
$$11$$
$$- 4$$
7

3.
$$15$$
$$- 6$$
9

4.
$$16$$
$$- 8$$
8

5.
$$14$$
$$- 7$$
7

6.
$$13$$
$$- 5$$
8

7.
$$17$$
$$- 9$$
8

8.
$$15$$
$$- 8$$
7

9.
$$18$$
$$- 9$$
9

10.
$$14$$
$$- 6$$
8

Write what or whom each underlined word stands for.
EXAMPLE:

The boys ran to the park. <u>They</u> ran to the park.

They = _____ **boys** _____

11. Carla and I like horses. We ride <u>them</u> every week.

them = ___ *horses* ___

12. My aunt called today. <u>She</u> is coming to visit us.

She = ___ *aunt* ___

13. I have a new bike. <u>It</u> is green.

it = ___ *bike* ___

14. I lost my umbrella. <u>It</u> is blue.

It = ___ *umbrella* ___

Read the sentence pairs. Write an X beside the sentence that happens first.

15. __X__ I planted seeds.

_____ The flowers grew.

16. __X__ Luke started his car.

_____ Luke drove his car.

17. _____ I put on my shoes.

__X__ I put on my socks.

18. __X__ We built a snowman.

_____ Our snowman melted.

19. _____ I brushed my teeth.

__X__ I put toothpaste on my toothbrush.

20. __X__ I climbed into bed.

_____ I fell asleep.

If you had to give away all of the things in your bedroom except for three things, which three things (other than your bed) would you keep? Why?

I would keep my desk
because, I can use it,
And my toys because
I can play with them.
Also my boxes because I
can put stuf in them

FITNESS FLASH: Touch your toes 10 times.

* See page ii.

PLACE STICKER HERE

Write > (greater than), < (less than), or = (equal to) to compare each expression.

EXAMPLE:

7 + 7 $<$ 15	1. 9 + 7 $=$ 16	2. 7 + 9 $<$ 18
8 + 6 $=$ 14	13 – 4 $<$ 10	17 – 9 $=$ 8
15 $>$ 1 + 9	4 + 6 $>$ 9	14 – 4 $=$ 10
3. 8 + 9 ◯ 9 + 8	4. 5 + 8 $=$ 6 + 7	5. 15 – 5 $>$ 13 – 4
11 – 4 ◯ 6 + 2	12 – 6 $<$ 6 + 6	18 – 8 $<$ 8 + 8
16 – 4 ◯ 3 + 10	10 + 1 $<$ 4 + 7	11 + 1 $=$ 6 + 6

Read each sentence. Circle the word or words that each underlined word stands for.

EXAMPLE:

(Carmella) will be home Friday. I will see <u>her</u> then.

6. The (fruit) is really good. <u>It</u> tastes sweet.

7. (José) and (Henry) ran fast. <u>They</u> won the race.

8. My (family) and (I) went on a picnic. <u>We</u> had a good time.

9. (Marisa) plays the piano. <u>She</u> plays very well.

10. I watered the (flowers) and put <u>them</u> on the bench.

11. (Daniel) took the dog inside. <u>He</u> took the cat there too.

DAY 15

Read the passage. Then, circle the answer that tells what the passage is about.

Birds

All birds are alike in some ways and different in others. They all have wings, but not all of them fly. Some are tame, and some are wild. Some birds sing. Some talk. Some are gentle. Others are not so gentle. Some birds fly very high and far. Others do not. Some birds are colorful while others are plain.

12. A. Some birds are tame. Others are not.

 B. All birds are strange and colorful.

 C. Birds are alike and different from each other.

Jellyfish Stretch and Glide

It is time to improve your flexibility! Pretend to be a jellyfish with long tentacles. Move around the room. Imagine that you are gliding through the ocean. Stretch your arms from your shoulders to your wrists. Flex each finger. Move your legs smoothly from your hips to your toes. Move your belly, back, and chest from left to right and front to back. Think about how you are moving. You should be slowly stretching several body parts at once. Add soft music or some ocean sounds as you glide toward better flexibility.

CHARACTER CHECK: What do you think is the most important good manner to have?

* See page ii.

PLACE STICKER HERE

Solve each problem.

1. Kara had 13 flowers. She sold 9 of them. How many flowers does she have left?

   4

2. Alexander can walk 2 miles in one hour. How many miles can he walk in two hours?

   4

3. Michael has 14 toy cars, and Todd has 10 toy cars. How many more cars does Michael have than Todd?

   4

4. Tisha has 9 teddy bears. Brittany has 6 dolls, and Shelby has 3 yo-yos. How many toys do the girls have in all?

   18

A verb is a word that often describes an action. If a verb is in the present tense, the action is happening now. Write the correct present-tense verb from the word bank to complete each sentence.

| finds ✓ | listens ✓ | rides ✓ | spills ✓ | works ✓ |

5. My mom ___listens___ to the radio in the morning.

6. Devon ___works___ at a store near his house.

7. Uncle Bill ___rides___ the bus to work.

8. Lilly ___spills___ her juice when she is in a hurry.

9. Dad ___finds___ pennies everywhere we go.

DAY 16

Read the passage. Then, answer the questions.

The Water Cycle

All water on Earth is part of the same cycle. Water starts out in oceans, lakes, and streams. When the sun heats the water, drops of water rise into the air. Water in this form is called water vapor. As the air cools, water droplets form clouds. When the clouds become too heavy with water, they produce rain, sleet, hail, or snow. The water falls back to Earth. Some of the water goes into the soil, where it helps plants grow. Some of the water falls into oceans, lakes, and streams. Then, the water cycle begins again. The next time you drink a glass of water, think about where it came from.

10. What is the main idea of this passage?

   A. All water on Earth moves through a cycle.

   B. Think about where your glass of water came from.

   C. Rain moves water back to Earth.

11. Where does the water cycle begin? _Oceans, lakes and streams_

12. What happens when the sun heats the water? _Drops of water rise into the air._

13. When do water droplets form clouds? _As the air cools._

14. What happens when the clouds become too heavy with water? _They produce rain, sleet, hail or snow._

15. Where does the rain go after it falls back to Earth? _Soil, oceans lakes and streams._

FACTOID: An ostrich's eye is bigger than its brain.

PLACE
STICKER
HERE

Add or subtract to solve each problem.

1. 84
    − 42
    42

2. 37
    − 13
    24

3. 69
    + 20
    89

4. 18
    − 4
    14

5. 57
    + 21
    78

6. 28
    − 16
    12

7. 24
    − 11
    13

8. 10
    − 10
    0

9. 23
    + 12
    35

10. 26
    + 22
    48

11. 43
    + 43
    86

12. 91
    + 6
    97

13. 15
    − 9
    6

14. 12
    + 2
    14

15. 49
    − 38
    11

Circle the present-tense verb in each sentence.

16. My dog Toby (runs) fast.

17. Aaron (thinks) about the question.

18. He (goes) to class.

19. Angelica (paints) a picture of flowers.

20. They (climb) to the top of the mountain.

21. Chad (builds) snowmen.

22. Jessica and I (go) to Camp Luna.

23. White clouds (float) in the blue sky.

24. Chris (watches) the parade from his window.

25. Jeremy (eats) lunch at that restaurant.

DAY 17

Read the stories. Decide what will happen next. Then, circle the letter beside the answer.

26. Amy was eating ice cream. Bethany bumped into Amy. What will happen next?

    A. Amy will drink some milk.

    B. Bethany will apologize.

    C. Amy will laugh.

27. Cody was playing tennis with Adam. The sun was very hot. The boys' faces were getting too much sun. What will happen next?

    A. Adam and Cody will go inside.

    B. Cody will walk to the pool.

    C. Cody and Adam will get cold.

Together, the letters *ph* make the /f/ sound. Read the sentences. Then, write the correct word from the word bank to complete each sentence.

| alphabet ✓ | amphibian ✓ | elephants ✓ | phone ✓ |

28. What is your _____ phone _____ number?

29. We saw _____ elephants _____ at the zoo.

30. Brad wrote the letters of the _____ alphabet _____ .

31. A frog is an _____ amphibian _____ .

FITNESS FLASH: Do arm circles for 30 seconds.

* See page ii.

PLACE STICKER HERE

Add to find each sum.

1. 324
    + 125
    449

2. 973
    + 24
    997

3. 777
    + 112
    889

4. 206
    + 132
    338

5. 111
    + 88
    199

6. 420
    + 337
    757

7. 623
    + 125
    748

8. 621
    + 126
    747

9. 230
    + 362
    592

10. 175
    + 113
    288

11. 803
    + 104
    907

12. 603
    + 292
    895

13. 600
    + 9
    609

14. 300
    + 500
    800

15. 821
    + 157
    978

If a verb is in the past tense, the action already happened. Add *-ed* or *-d* to a word to show past tense. Add *-ed* when the word ends in a consonant. Add *-d* when the word ends in a vowel.

EXAMPLE:

wait **ed**

16. laugh **ed**

17. skate **d**

18. clean **ed**

19. jump **ed**

20. wash **ed**

21. rain **ed**

22. save **d**

23. time **d**

24. bake **d**

25. work **ed**

26. mask **ed**

27. hope

28. talk **ed**

29. love **d**

DAY 18

Read each sentence. Then, answer the questions.

30. J. T. is going to David's volleyball game.

    Who is going to the game? _J.T._

    Whose game is it? _David's_

31. Evan is reading Kendra's book.

    Who does the book belong to? _Kendra_

    Who is reading? _Evan_

Read each sentence. Then, write the correct word from the word bank to complete each sentence.

| quarter ✓ | queen ✓ | question ✓ | quiet ✓ | quilt ✓ | Squeeze ✓ |

32. _Squeeze_ the oranges to make juice.

33. I have a colorful _quilt_ on my bed.

34. Shhh, be very _quiet_ in the library.

35. The piece of candy cost a _quarter_.

36. The king and the _queen_ sit on thrones.

37. I would like to ask a _question_.

FACTOID: Almonds come from the same plant family as peaches and roses.

PLACE
STICKER
HERE

Subtract to find each difference.

1. $\begin{array}{r} 758 \\ -126 \\ \hline \end{array}$ 632

2. $\begin{array}{r} 410 \\ -310 \\ \hline \end{array}$ 100

3. $\begin{array}{r} 894 \\ -251 \\ \hline \end{array}$ 643

4. $\begin{array}{r} 978 \\ -165 \\ \hline \end{array}$ 813

5. $\begin{array}{r} 879 \\ -704 \\ \hline \end{array}$ 175

6. $\begin{array}{r} 785 \\ -223 \\ \hline \end{array}$ 562

7. $\begin{array}{r} 583 \\ -161 \\ \hline \end{array}$ 422

8. $\begin{array}{r} 957 \\ -140 \\ \hline \end{array}$ 817

9. $\begin{array}{r} 683 \\ -611 \\ \hline \end{array}$ 072

10. $\begin{array}{r} 896 \\ -840 \\ \hline \end{array}$ 56

11. $\begin{array}{r} 686 \\ -255 \\ \hline \end{array}$ 431

12. $\begin{array}{r} 349 \\ -104 \\ \hline \end{array}$ 245

13. $\begin{array}{r} 867 \\ -36 \\ \hline \end{array}$ 831

14. $\begin{array}{r} 539 \\ -39 \\ \hline \end{array}$ 500

15. $\begin{array}{r} 767 \\ -10 \\ \hline \end{array}$ 757

Circle the past-tense verb to complete each sentence.

16. We (pick, **picked**) strawberries this morning.

17. I (smile, **smiled**) when I saw my friend.

18. Maria (search, **searched**) for her pencil.

19. She (**rode**, ride) the bus to school.

20. I (ask, **asked**) Dad if I could go to the museum.

21. Grandma (mend, **mended**) the tear in my shirt.

22. We (mix, **mixed**) oil and vinegar to dress the salad.

DAY 19

Read the poem. Then, answer the questions.

My Shadow

I have a little shadow that goes in and out with me,

And what can be the use of him is more than I can see.

He is very, very like me from the heels up to the head;

And I see him jump before me, when I jump into my bed.

– Robert Louis Stevenson

23. What does the boy's shadow do when he jumps into bed? _It jumps before him._

24. Who does the boy's shadow look like? _the boy_

25. Where does the boy's shadow go? _every where he goes_

26. When do you see your shadow? _in the sun_

Read each word. Then, circle the letter or letters that are silent.

27. Ⓦrist

28. thum(b)

29. (k)hee

30. (k)not

31. (k)ni(gh)t

32. com(b)

FITNESS FLASH: Do 10 shoulder shrugs.

* See page ii.

PLACE STICKER HERE

Add or subtract to solve each problem.

1. 573
    − 132
    441

2. 832
    + 23
    855

3. 153
    + 210
    363

4. 637
    − 224
    413

5. 638
    − 532
    106

6.   34
    + 25
    59

7. 263
    + 13
    276

8. 508
    − 305
    203

9. 337
    + 231
    568

10. 544
    + 234
    778

11. 872
    + 121
    993

12. 684
    + 102
    786

13. 912
    + 87
    999

14. 400
    + 500
    900

15. 505
    + 292
    797

Write each verb on the correct ladder.
EXAMPLE:

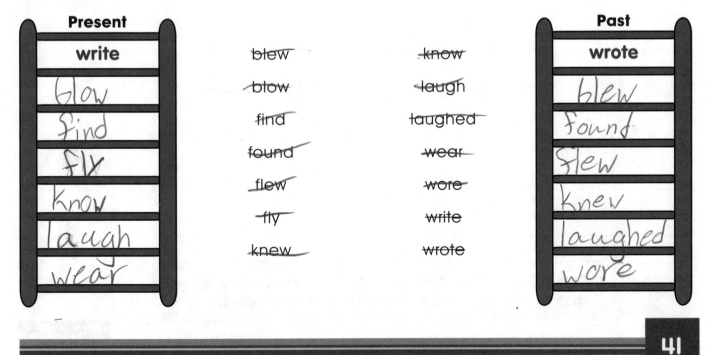

Present

| write |
| blow |
| find |
| fix |
| know |
| laugh |
| wear |

blew
blow
find
found
flew
fly
knew

know
laugh
laughed
wear
wore
write
wrote

Past

| wrote |
| blew |
| found |
| flew |
| knew |
| laughed |
| wore |

Read each sentence. Write _R_ if the sentence tells something that is real. Write _F_ if the sentence tells something that is a fantasy.

16. _F_ Jennifer wears a watch on her nose.

17. _R_ A robin flew to the branch in the tree.

18. _R_ Roberto helped his father paint the fence.

19. _F_ Danielle heard two trees talking.

20. _F_ Kyle eats his lunch with a hammer and a saw.

21. _R_ Kayla has two pillows on her bed.

22. _F_ Birds use their beaks to fly.

23. _R_ Derek lost a baby tooth last night.

24. _F_ That cow is driving a bus!

25. _F_ The moose gave the frog a cookie.

Imagine that you are designing a T-shirt for a sports team, a school club, or a special event. Then, draw and color your shirt on another sheet of paper. Write a paragraph about your shirt.

I would make a shirt that has my name and lots of colors.

CHARACTER CHECK: Make a list of three things that you can do to calm down when you are upset.

PLACE STICKER HERE

The Impossible Balloon

Can you inflate a balloon in a bottle?

Materials:

- balloon
- plastic bottle (2-liter)

Procedure:

With an adult, put the balloon inside the bottle while holding on to the mouth of the balloon. Stretch the mouth of the balloon over the mouth of the bottle so that it stays in place. Then, put your lips on the bottle. Try to inflate the balloon.

What's This All About?

When you stretch the balloon over the mouth of the bottle, it seals the bottle. No air can get in or out of the bottle. As you try to inflate the balloon, it pushes against the air inside the bottle. The air pushes on the balloon and does not let the balloon get any bigger. Air takes up space and can push things that push it.

More Fun Ideas to Try:

- Try different sizes of bottles to see if you can inflate the balloon in other bottles.
- Try round balloons or long balloons. Before you try the experiment, write what you think might happen.
- Have an adult punch a small hole in the bottom of a bottle. Try the experiment with this bottle.

* See page ii.

BONUS

Fluid Motion

Will the same object move at different speeds through different fluids?

Speed is the term used to describe how fast an object moves. To calculate speed, divide the distance the object moved by how much time it took to move.

Materials:

- 2 identical jars
- vegetable oil
- stopwatch
- calculator
- water
- two identical marbles
- metric ruler

Procedure:

Fill one jar with water and one jar with vegetable oil.

Hold one marble so that the bottom of the marble touches the top of the vegetable oil. Drop the marble. Use the stopwatch to record the time in seconds that it takes the marble to reach the bottom of the jar. Then, use the ruler to measure the distance the marble travels. Record your data in the chart.

Follow the same procedure for the second marble and the jar of water. Record your data in the chart.

Divide the distance that each marble traveled by the number of seconds it took for that marble to drop. Use a calculator if you need help.

Measurements			
Fluid	Distance	Time	Speed
vegetable oil			
water			

1. Which marble travelled faster? _____

2. What is the difference between the speed of the first marble and the speed of the second marble? _____

X Marks the Spot

Follow the directions to find the treasure. Draw an X where the treasure is buried. Then, answer the question.

- Start in the Red River Valley.

- Go northeast through Lake Lavender to the Black Forest.

- Go northeast to the Evergreen Forest.

- Travel north to the Purple Mountains.

- Cross the Red River to the Blue Mountains.

- Go south, but do not cross the Red River again.

- The treasure is buried here.

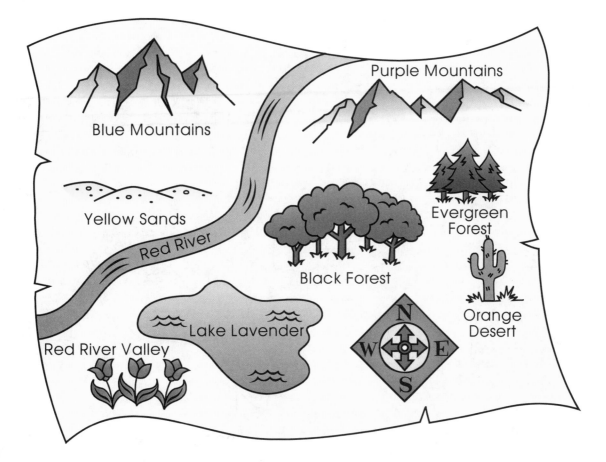

Where is the treasure buried? _____

BONUS

What's the Key?

A map key tells what the symbols on a map stand for. Use the map key to find the objects listed.

1. Circle each city.

2. Draw a square around each baseball park.

3. Draw an X on the state capital.

4. Draw a triangle around the airport.

5. Underline the parks.

6. Draw a star on each university.

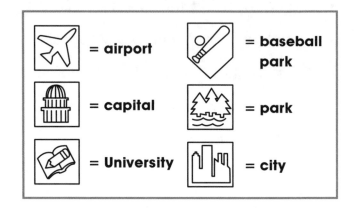

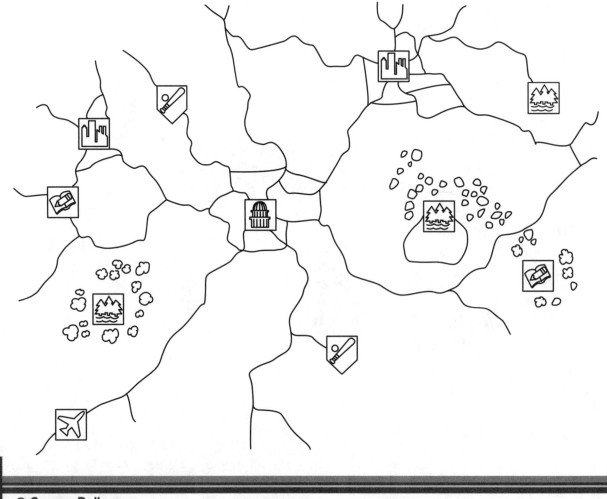

Brent's Street Map

Brent has a street map to help him find his way around his new town. A street map shows where businesses, homes, and other places are located. Look at the street map and answer the questions.

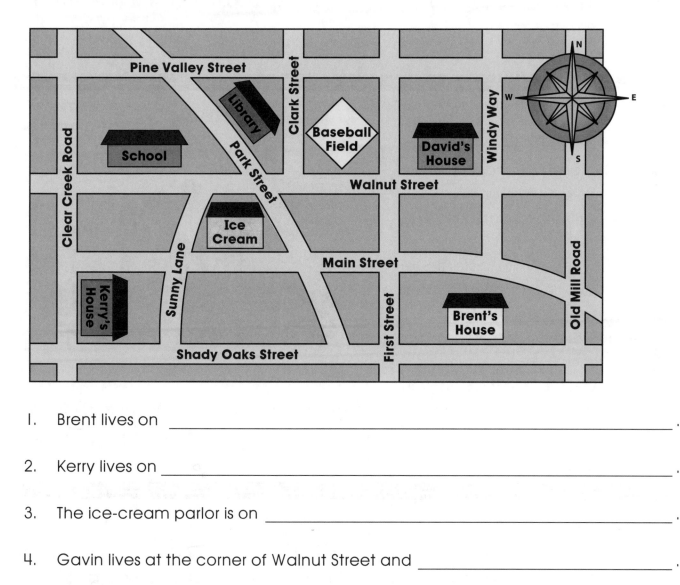

1. Brent lives on _____.

2. Kerry lives on _____.

3. The ice-cream parlor is on _____.

4. Gavin lives at the corner of Walnut Street and _____.

5. The school is on _____.

6. What two streets could Brent take to get to the library?

   _____

Take It Outside!

Summer is a great time to read outdoors. Choose a favorite book and find a shady spot to relax and read. Bring a pencil and notebook too. As you read, write your thoughts, interesting facts, and any new words that you learn. Review your notes at the end of the summer.

Plant a garden! Ask an adult to help you find a large container or choose a spot in the yard. With an adult, go online or visit the library to learn about plants that grow well in your region. Get seeds (vegetable, flower, or herb), some good soil, and water. Plant the seeds. Then, tend your garden by watering and weeding as needed. Record what you planted and when you planted it so that you  can chart the growth of your plants. By the end of summer, you will have a garden to be proud of!

Head outside with a notebook and pencil. For five minutes, observe what is happening around you. Make a list of the actions you observe, such as a dog barking, a bird flying, a grasshopper jumping, or a person talking. When you are finished, count the number of different verbs on your list. There are so many verbs to observe!

* See page ii.

Monthly Goals

Think of three goals to set for yourself this month. For example, you may want to exercise for 20 minutes each day. Write your goals on the lines and review them with an adult.

Place a sticker next to each goal that you complete. Feel proud that you have met your goals!

1. _To practice soccer._ PLACE STICKER HERE

2. _To do good in school._ PLACE STICKER HERE

3. _Take care of my dog._ PLACE STICKER HERE

Word List

The following words are used in this section. They are good words for you to know. Read each word. Use a dictionary to look up each word that you do not know. Then, write two sentences. Use a word from the word list in each sentence.

advertising   nectar

cabin   popular

illustrated   published

integrity   seasons

molt   tropical

1. _We stayed in a cabin._

2. _She illustrated and published the book._

Introduction to Strength

This section includes fitness and character development activities that focus on strength. These activities are designed to get you moving and thinking about strengthening your body and your character.

Physical Strength

Like flexibility, strength is important for good health. You may think that a strong person is someone who can lift a lot of weight. However, strength is more than the ability to pick up heavy things. Strength is built over time. You are stronger now than you were in preschool. What are some activities that you can do now that you could not do then?

You can gain strength through everyday activities and many fun exercises. Carry grocery bags to build your arms. Ride a bike to strengthen your legs. Swim to strengthen your whole body. Exercises such as push-ups and chin-ups are also great strength builders.

Set goals this summer to improve your strength. Base your goals on activities that you enjoy. Talk about your goals with an adult. As you meet your goals, set new ones. Celebrate your stronger body!

Strength of Character

As you build your physical strength, work on your inner strength too. Having a strong character means standing up for what you know is right, even if others do not agree.

You can show inner strength in many ways, such as being honest, standing up for someone who needs your help, and putting your best efforts into every task. It is not always easy to show inner strength. Can you think of a time when you used inner strength to handle a situation, such as being teased by another child at the park?

Improve your inner strength over the summer. Think about ways you can show strength of character, such as showing good sportsmanship in your baseball league. Reflect on your positive growth. Be proud of your strong character!

Add to find each sum. Add the numbers in the ones place first and then the numbers in the tens place.

EXAMPLE:

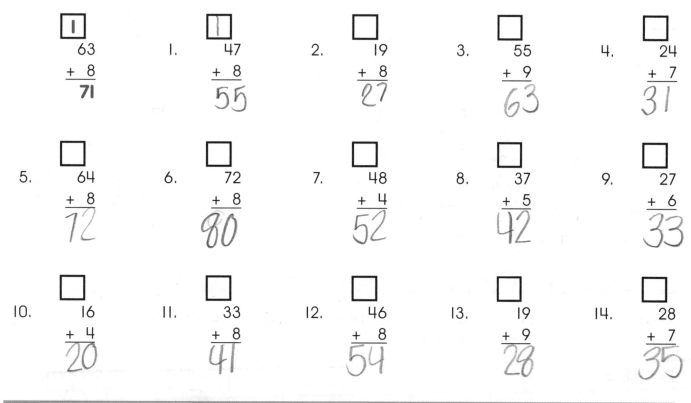

| | 63
+ 8
71 | 1. | 47
+ 8
55 | 2. | 19
+ 8
27 | 3. | 55
+ 9
63 | 4. | 24
+ 7
31 |

| 5. | 64
+ 8
72 | 6. | 72
+ 8
80 | 7. | 48
+ 4
52 | 8. | 37
+ 5
42 | 9. | 27
+ 6
33 |

| 10. | 16
+ 4
20 | 11. | 33
+ 8
41 | 12. | 46
+ 8
54 | 13. | 19
+ 9
28 | 14. | 28
+ 7
35 |

Draw a line to match each present-tense verb with its past-tense form.

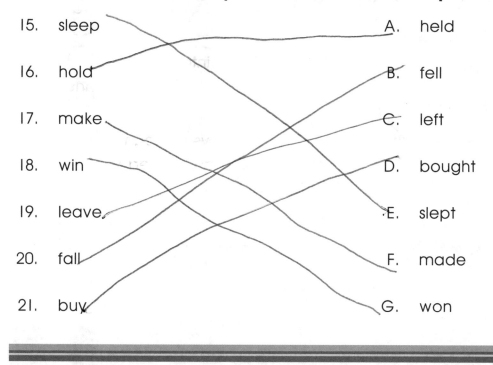

15. sleep   A. held

16. hold   B. fell

17. make   C. left

18. win   D. bought

19. leave   E. slept

20. fall   F. made

21. buy   G. won

DAY 1

Record how many vowels, syllables, and vowel sounds are in each word. Remember: there are as many syllables in a word as there are vowel sounds.

△ = number of vowels □ = number of syllables ○ = number of vowel sounds

EXAMPLE:

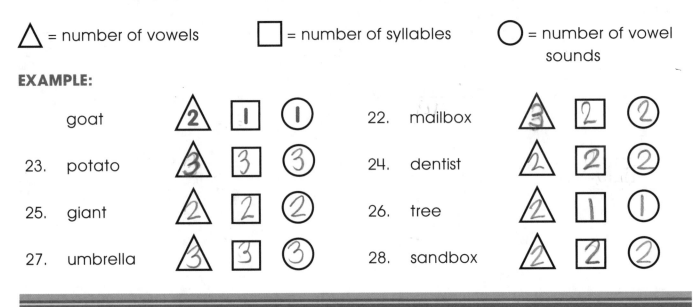

goat △2 □1 ○1

23. potato △3 □3 ○3
25. giant △2 □2 ○2
27. umbrella △3 □3 ○3

22. mailbox △3 □2 ○2
24. dentist △2 □2 ○2
26. tree △2 □1 ○1
28. sandbox △2 □2 ○2

Read the sentences. Look at each underlined word. Then, color in the circle to tell if the word is spelled correctly or incorrectly.

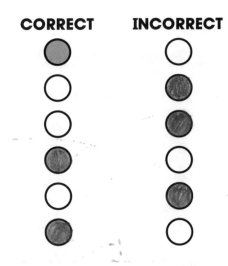

EXAMPLE: We <u>ate</u> toast with jam on it.

29. We <u>wint</u> to the store for some bread and milk.
30. The dog will hunt for his <u>boone</u>.
31. We will <u>plant</u> our garden.
32. The <u>keng</u> asked the queen to dance.
33. <u>Think</u> of a good name for a cat.

CORRECT INCORRECT

FACTOID: Birds could never be astronauts. They need gravity in order to swallow!

Subtract to find each difference. Subtract the numbers in the ones place first and then the numbers in the tens place.

EXAMPLE:

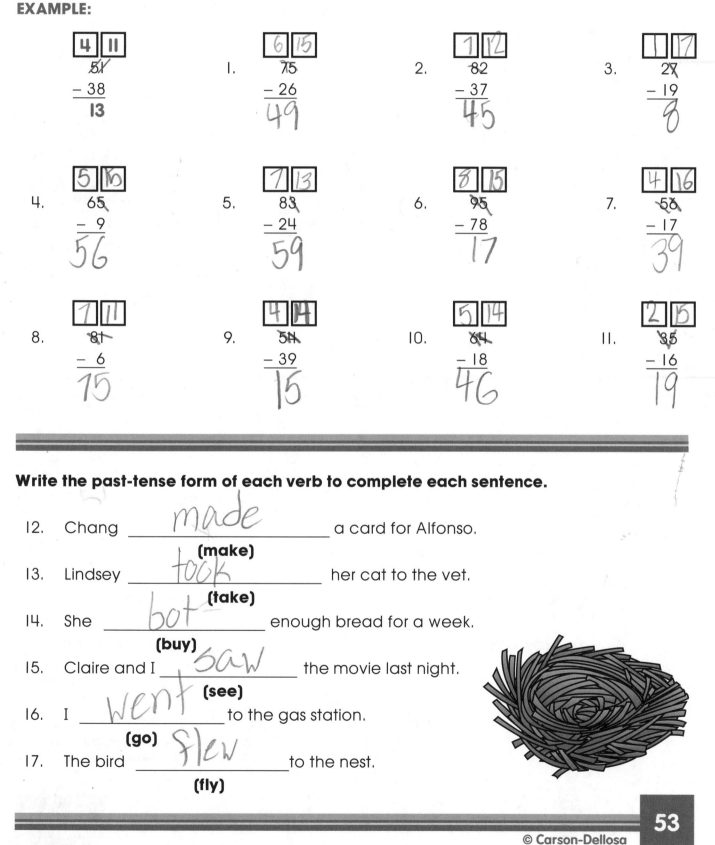

|4|11|
5̶1̶
− 38
13

1. |6|15|
7̶5̶
− 26
49

2. |7|12|
8̶2̶
− 37
45

3. | |17|
2̶7̶
− 19
8

4. |5|15|
6̶5̶
− 9
56

5. |7|13|
8̶3̶
− 24
59

6. |8|15|
9̶5̶
− 78
17

7. |4|16|
5̶6̶
− 17
39

8. |7|11|
8̶1̶
− 6
15

9. |4|14|
5̶4̶
− 39
15

10. |5|14|
6̶4̶
− 18
46

11. |2|15|
3̶5̶
− 16
19

Write the past-tense form of each verb to complete each sentence.

12. Chang _____made_____ a card for Alfonso.
(make)

13. Lindsey _____took_____ her cat to the vet.
(take)

14. She _____bot_____ enough bread for a week.
(buy)

15. Claire and I _____saw_____ the movie last night.
(see)

16. I _____went_____ to the gas station.
(go)

17. The bird _____flew_____ to the nest.
(fly)

DAY 2

Read the poem. Then, answer the questions.

Sing a Song of Summer

Sing a song of summer
with arms stretched open wide.
Run in the sunshine.
Play all day outside.

Hold on to the summer
as long as you may.
Autumn will come quickly
and shorten the day.

Play in the water.
Roll in the grass.
It won't be long now
before you'll be in class.

18. Which sentence tells the main idea of the poem?

    (A.) Enjoy summer while it lasts.   B.   Summer gets too hot.

    C.   School starts in the autumn.   D.   It is fun to sing songs.

19. What season comes after summer?

    A.   winter   B.   spring

    (C.) autumn   D.   October

20. Write an X beside each thing you can do in the summer.

    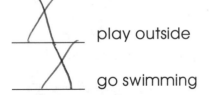 play outside   _____ rake leaves

    _____ go swimming   _____ build a snowman

FITNESS FLASH: Do five push-ups.

* See page ii.

PLACE
STICKER
HERE

Add or subtract to solve each problem.

1.   33
   + 18
   51

2.   62
   − 28
   34

3.   19
   + 20
   39

4.   53
   − 5
   48

5.   58
   + 24
   82

6.   44
   − 18
   26

7.   34
   − 9
   27

8.   72
   + 9
   81

9.   75
   − 47
   28

10.   81
   + 11
   92

11.   31
   − 21
   10

12.   28
   + 14
   42

13.   46
   − 6
   40

14.   31
   − 16
   15

15.   54
   + 27
   81

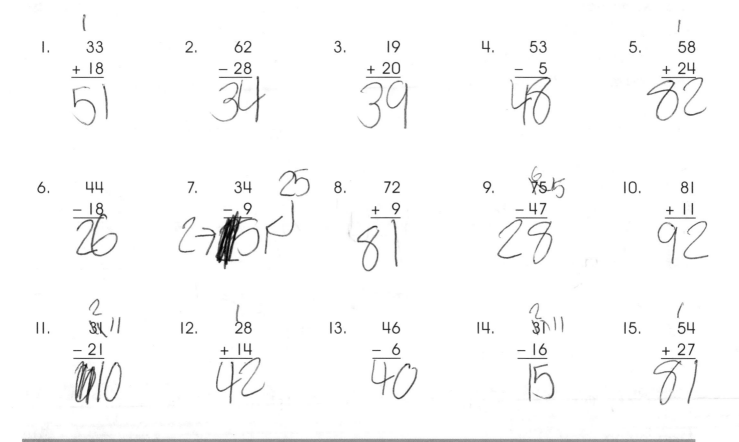

Write *am*, *is*, or *are* to complete each sentence.

16.   I ____**am**____ the tallest girl on the team.

17.   My lunch ____**is**____ in my backpack.

18.   We ____**are**____ in line for the roller coaster.

19.   I ____**am**____ ready to go swimming.

20.   Jonah's friends ____**are**____ laughing at a joke.

21.   Aunt Ebony ____**is**____ listening to music.

22.   We ____**are**____ painting the room blue.

DAY 3

Write a synonym from the word bank to take the place of the underlined word in each sentence.

| creek ✓ | largest ✓ | leaped ✓ | giggling ✓ | middle ✓ | yell ✓ |

23. He jumped over the mud puddle. _leaped_

24. Let's clap and shout for our team. _yell_

25. Were the children laughing? _giggling_

26. He is riding the biggest bike. _largest_

27. We saw fish in the stream. ~~cree~~ _creek_

28. Stand in the center of the circle. _middle_

Monkeying Around

With an adult, visit a playground. Find the monkey bars. Begin by swinging by your arms from bar to bar. If you need practice, set a goal such as swing across, rest, and go back. If you are very good at swinging across the bars, see how many times you can go back and forth. You are not just monkeying around! You are improving your upper body strength!

FACTOID: Grown-ups blink about 10 times a minute, but babies blink only once or twice a minute.

* See page ii.

Add to find each sum.

EXAMPLE:

☐1				
32	1. 28	2. 70	3. 44	4. 57
11	14	99	2	32
+ 19	+ 4	+ 12	+ 38	+ 89
62	46	181	84	178

5. 81	6. 22	7. 67	8. 81	9. 74
38	9	45	8	33
+ 64	+ 19	+ 15	+ 8	+ 17
183	50	127	97	124

Write *am*, *is*, or *are* to complete each sentence.

10. I ____am____ going to the library.

11. You ____are____ running to Anton's house.

12. I ____am____ playing my favorite game.

13. Mom ____is____ sitting in the front row.

14. You ____are____ the winner!

15. I ____am____ looking at the ocean.

16. Juan ____is____ trying to catch a baseball.

17. The rabbit's fur ____is____ soft.

18. The clothes ____are____ on sale.

DAY 4

Write the words under the correct heading. The first one has been done for you.

	Synonyms (same)	Antonyms (opposite)	Homophones (sound alike)
would, wood		high, low	would, wood
19. high, low		~~~~	
20. pile, heap		pile, heap	
21. weight, wait			weight, wait
22. blend, mix	blend, mix		
23. empty, full		empty, full	
24. rain, reign			rain, reign
25. cool, warm		cool, warm	

Unscramble the words to complete each sentence.

Matter is what things are made of. It has three forms:

_____gas_____ , _____solid_____ , and _____liquid_____ .
(sga)   (osdil)   (dqiiul)

_____Mater_____ can be big or little and soft or hard.
(tertaM)

Ice is a ___solid___ . When it melts, it is a ___liquid___ .
(dliso)   (ildqui)

___Gas___ is all around you, but you cannot see it.
(asG)

FITNESS FLASH: Do 10 lunges.

* See page ii.

Use a red pencil to check the problems. Write a √ beside each correct answer. Write an X beside each incorrect answer.

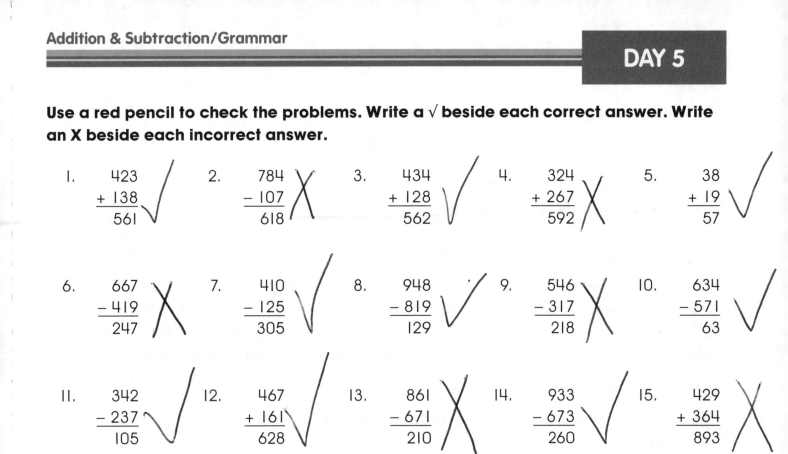

1. 423
    + 138
    ——
    561 √

2. 784
    − 107
    ——
    618 X

3. 434
    + 128
    ——
    562 √

4. 324
    + 267
    ——
    592 X

5. 38
    + 19
    ——
    57 √

6. 667
    − 419
    ——
    247 X

7. 410
    − 125
    ——
    305 √

8. 948
    − 819
    ——
    129 √

9. 546
    − 317
    ——
    218 X

10. 634
    − 571
    ——
    63 √

11. 342
    − 237
    ——
    105 √

12. 467
    + 161
    ——
    628 √

13. 861
    − 671
    ——
    210 X

14. 933
    − 673
    ——
    260 √

15. 429
    + 364
    ——
    893 X

Write *has* or *have* to complete each sentence.

16. We _____have_____ fun plans for this summer.

17. My mom _____has_____ Friday off.

18. My dad _____has_____ a new book.

19. The girl _____has_____ a hat.

20. Lia and I _____have_____ fruit in our lunches.

21. The doghouses _____have_____ new roofs.

22. His sister _____has_____ dance shoes.

23. The club _____has_____ many members.

DAY 5

Read the passage. Then, answer the questions.

Mercer Mayer

Mercer Mayer's books can be found in many libraries and bookstores. He has both written and illustrated books. Some of his most popular books include *There's a Nightmare in My Closet*; *Liza Lou and the Yeller Belly Swamp*; *Just for You*; and *A Boy, a Dog, and a Frog*. He likes to write about things that happened to him as a child.

Mercer Mayer was born on December 30, 1943, in Arkansas. When he was 13, he moved to Hawaii with his family. After high school, he studied art. Then, he worked for an advertising company in New York. He published his first book in 1967. He and his wife work together on the Little Critter stories. Now, he works from his home in Connecticut.

24. This passage is called a biography. Based on what you read, what do you think a biography is?

   A. a made-up story about a character from a book

   B. a true story that tells about the life of a real person

   C. a short, funny story

Write *T* for statements that are true. Write *F* for statements that are false.

25. _F_ Mercer Mayer is a character in a book.

26. _T_ Mercer Mayer writes about things that happened to him as a child.

27. _T_ Mercer Mayer lived in many different places.

28. _F_ Mercer Mayer never worked in New York.

CHARACTER CHECK: Brainstorm a list of ways that you can show responsibility. Post your list somewhere that you will see it often.

Write the time shown on each clock.

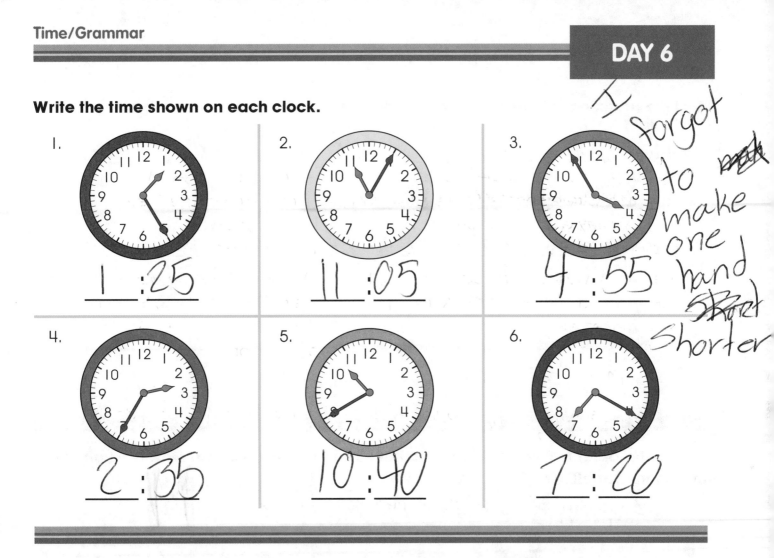

1. 1:25

2. 11:05

3. 4:55

I forgot to make one hand shorter

4. 2:35

5. 10:40

6. 7:20

The suffix -ing is added to a verb to show that something is happening now. Read each word. Then, add -ing to the word.

7. go _ing_

8. say _ing_

9. do _ing_

10. sleep _ing_

11. walk _ing_

12. read _ing_

13. paint _ing_

14. work _ing_

15. eat _ing_

16. spell _ing_

17. cook _ing_

18. watch _ing_

DAY 6

Add the prefix *un-* or *re-* to each word. Then, write the meaning of each new word.

19. sure   un
    ~~unsursh~~ unsure

20. happy   un
    unhappy

21. like   ~~un~~ un
    unlike

22. write   re
    rewrite

23. tell   re
    retell

24. print   re
    re print

Which character from a book that you have read is most like you? How are you and this character alike?

Annie from the Magic Tree House, because she likes ~~books~~ books

FACTOID: Koala fingerprints look similar to human fingerprints.

Draw hands on each clock to show the correct time.

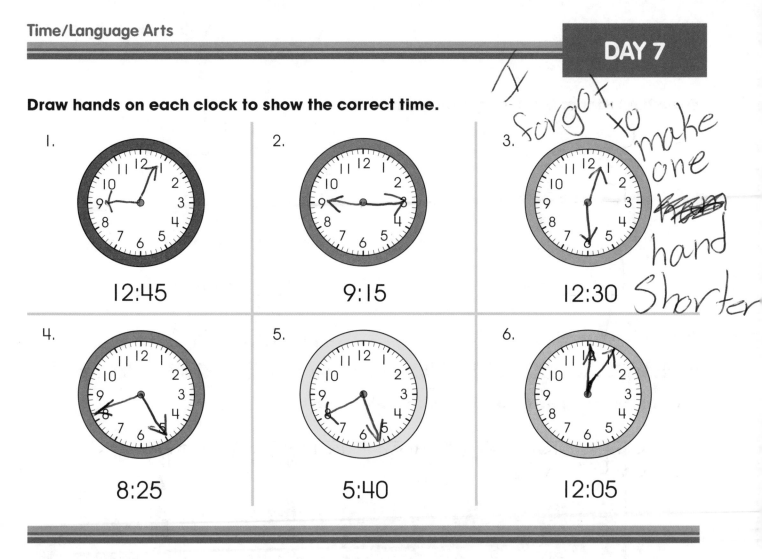

I forgot to make one hand shorter

1. 12:45
2. 9:15
3. 12:30
4. 8:25
5. 5:40
6. 12:05

Add the suffixes -ed and -ing to each base word. You may need to drop letters from or add letters to some words before adding the suffixes.

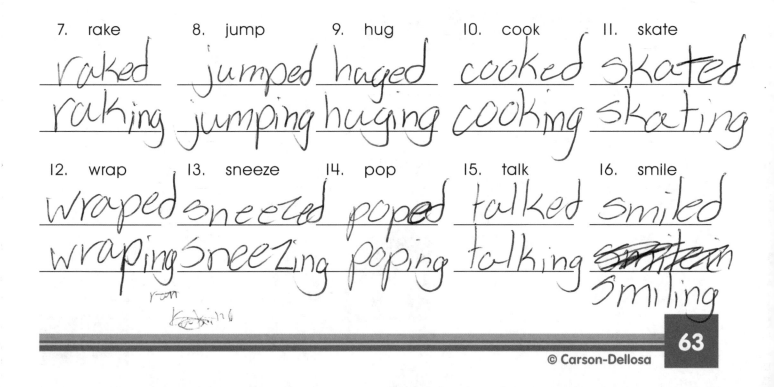

7. rake — raked, raking
8. jump — jumped, jumping
9. hug — huged, huging
10. cook — cooked, cooking
11. skate — skated, skating
12. wrap — wraped, wraping
13. sneeze — sneezed, sneezing
14. pop — poped, poping
15. talk — talked, talking
16. smile — smiled, smiling

DAY 7

Write the letter of the correct definition next to each word.

17. __C__ cheerful

18. __E__ sleepless

19. __D__ colorful

20. __B__ sunless

21. __A__ helpful

A. ready to help

B. without sun

C. very cheery

D. having many colors

E. not able to sleep

Look at the map and map key to answer the questions.

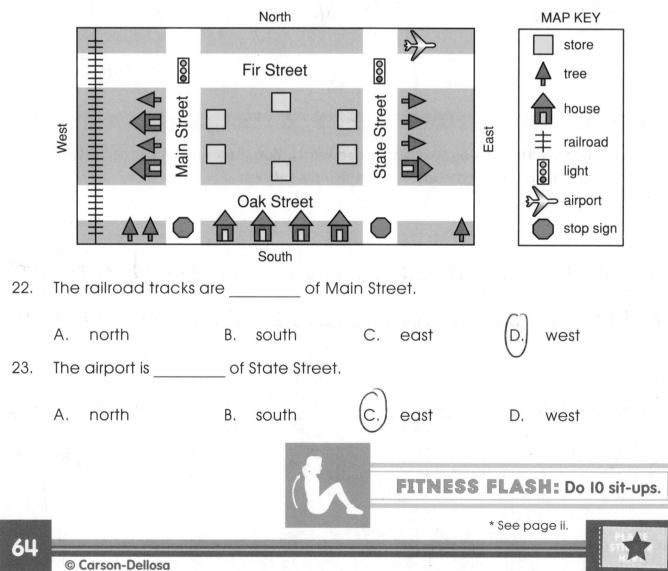

22. The railroad tracks are _____ of Main Street.

   A. north   B. south   C. east   D. west

23. The airport is _____ of State Street.

   A. north   B. south   C. east   D. west

FITNESS FLASH: Do 10 sit-ups.

* See page ii.

Draw hands on each clock to show the correct time.

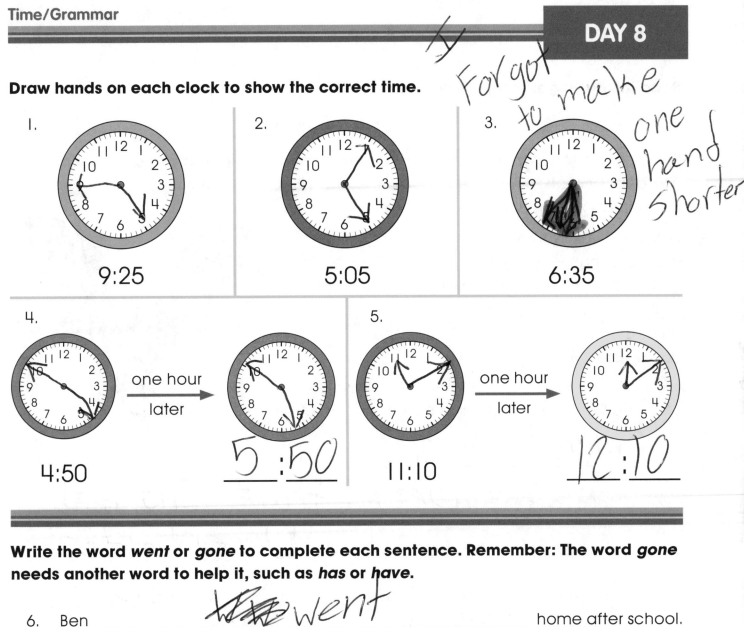

I Forgot to make one hand shorter

1. 9:25

2. 5:05

3. 6:35

4. 4:50 → one hour later → 5:50

5. 11:10 → one hour later → 12:10

Write the word *went* or *gone* to complete each sentence. Remember: The word *gone* needs another word to help it, such as *has* or *have*.

6. Ben _____ went _____ home after school.

7. Jessi has _____ gone _____ shopping for a new coat.

8. Deanna _____ went _____ with Andrew to play.

9. We will be _____ gone _____ on vacation all week.

10. My mother _____ went _____ to work this morning.

DAY 8

Read the passage. Then, answer the questions.

Nightly Navigators

Bats help people in many ways. Most bats eat insects at night. This helps to keep the number of insects low. Bats eat mosquitoes, mayflies, and moths. Bats also pollinate and spread the seeds of many tropical trees.

Bats are the only flying mammals on Earth. There are more than 900 kinds of bats. Some bats are only 1.3 inches (3.3 centimeters) long. Some are more than 16 inches (40 centimeters) long. Most bats eat only insects. Some bats eat fruit and the nectar of flowers.

11.   How many different kinds of bats are there?

more than 900

12.   What do bats eat? insects, fruit and nectar

13.   How large can some types of bats grow? 40 centimeters

14.   Write three ways that bats help people. eat insects, spread seeds, and pollinate

15.   Name three types of insects that bats eat. mosquitoes, mayflies and moths

FACTOID: Your heart is about the same size as your fist.

PLACE STICKER HERE

Circle the coins to equal each amount shown.

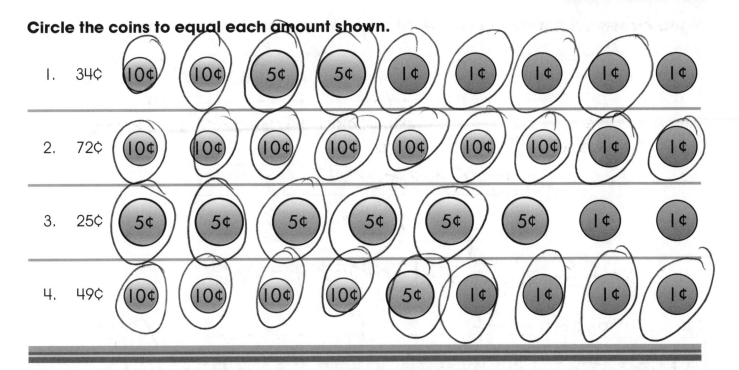

1. 34¢ 10¢ 10¢ 5¢ 5¢ 1¢ 1¢ 1¢ 1¢ 1¢

2. 72¢ 10¢ 10¢ 10¢ 10¢ 10¢ 10¢ 10¢ 1¢ 1¢

3. 25¢ 5¢ 5¢ 5¢ 5¢ 5¢ 5¢ 1¢ 1¢

4. 49¢ 10¢ 10¢ 10¢ 10¢ 5¢ 1¢ 1¢ 1¢ 1¢

Write a word from each box to complete each sentence.

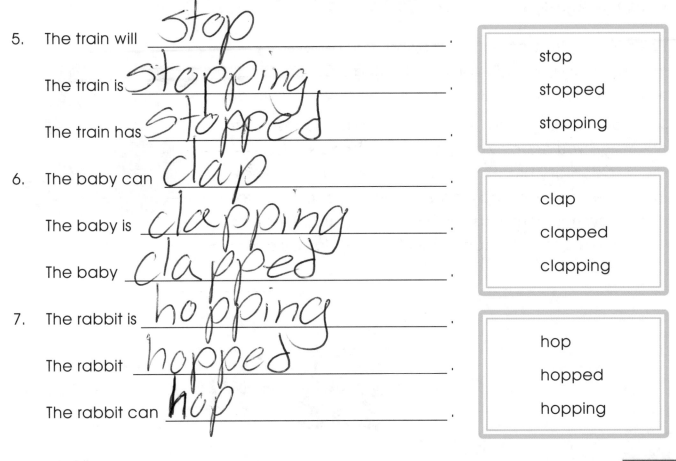

5. The train will _stop_ .

   The train is _stopping_ .

   The train has _stopped_ .

| stop |
| stopped |
| stopping |

6. The baby can _clap_ .

   The baby is _clapping_ .

   The baby _clapped_ .

| clap |
| clapped |
| clapping |

7. The rabbit is _hopping_ .

   The rabbit _hopped_ .

   The rabbit can _hop_ .

| hop |
| hopped |
| hopping |

DAY 9

Write a compound word from the word bank to complete each sentence.

barefoot ✓   classmates ✓   dinnertime ✓   seashells ✓   springtime ✓

8. Jordan is one of my favorite _classmates_.

9. Josh likes to walk _barefoot_.

10. It rains a lot during _springtime_.

11. Our family ate spaghetti at _dinnertime_.

12. I like to collect _seashells_ at the beach.

A Sticky Situation

Having integrity means showing what you believe through your actions. Read the following situation. On a separate sheet of paper, write about what you would do.

Situation: You know that it is important to be honest. One day when you are playing at your best friend's house, she accidentally breaks her mom's cookie jar. She glues the pieces together and places it back on a table. Later in the day, her mom finds you two playing and questions both of you about the cookie jar. What would you do?

FITNESS FLASH: Do 10 squats.

* See page ii.

Count the money. Write each amount.

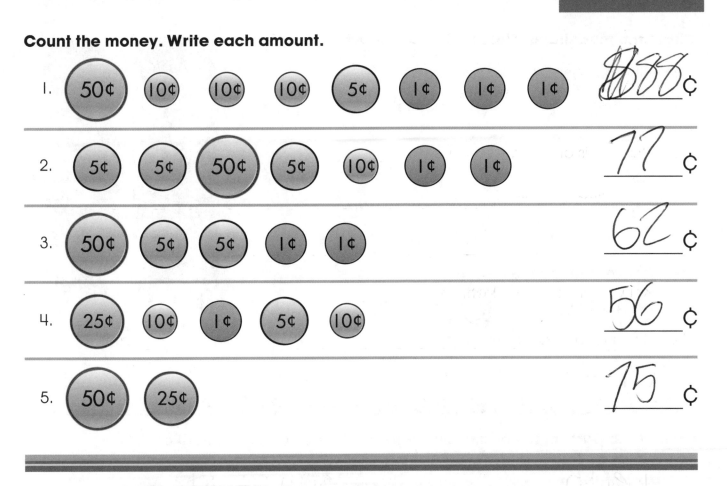

1. 50¢ 10¢ 10¢ 10¢ 5¢ 1¢ 1¢ 1¢ $88 ¢

2. 5¢ 5¢ 50¢ 5¢ 10¢ 1¢ 1¢   77 ¢

3. 50¢ 5¢ 5¢ 1¢ 1¢   62 ¢

4. 25¢ 10¢ 1¢ 5¢ 10¢   56 ¢

5. 50¢ 25¢   75 ¢

Cross out each incorrectly used or misspelled word in the journal entry. Write the correct word above it.

September 14, 2011

Yesterday, we learn about colors in art. We make a color wheel. We found out that

there is three basic colors. They are called primary colors. Red, yellow, and blue

are primary colors. Primary colors mix to make other colors. Red and yellow makes

orange. Yellow and blue make green. Blue and red make purple. Orange, green,

and purple is secondary colors.

DAY 10

Circle the meaning of each underlined word.

6. She has on a <u>dark</u> purple dress.

    A. night   B. not light

7. We were <u>safe</u> on the rock.

    A. without danger   B. place to keep things

8. Fernando had to be home before <u>dark</u>.

    A. morning   B. night

9. I took a <u>trip</u> to the museum.

    A. a visit   B. to stumble

10. The <u>bank</u> closes at five o'clock.

    A. place where money is kept   B. a steep hill

Look at the parts of the bird. Then, write the words in alphabetical order.

11. beak

12. eye

13. feet

14. tail

15. wing

beak
eye
wing
tail
feet

CHARACTER CHECK: Look up *unique* in a dictionary. How are you unique?

Count the groups of money in each problem. Draw an X on the group that is worth more.

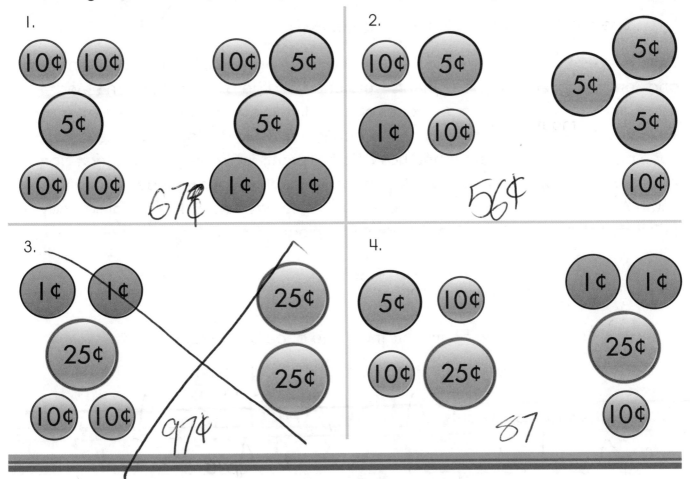

1. 10¢ 10¢ 10¢ 5¢
   5¢ 5¢
   10¢ 10¢ 67¢ 1¢ 1¢

2. 10¢ 5¢ 5¢
   1¢ 10¢ 5¢ 5¢
   56¢ 10¢

3. 1¢ 1¢ 25¢
   25¢
   10¢ 10¢ 97¢ 25¢

4. 5¢ 10¢ 1¢ 1¢
   10¢ 25¢ 25¢
   87 10¢

Adjectives describe nouns. Some adjectives describe how things look or sound. Some adjectives describe how things feel or taste. Write the best adjective from the word bank to complete each sentence.

| rainy ✓ | equal ✓ | low ✓ | tiny ✓ |

5. I put an _____ equal _____ amount of soup in my bowl and yours.

6. There is a _____ tiny _____ bug on the leaf.

7. Latoya stepped over the _____ low _____ wall.

8. She saw a rainbow in the sky on the _____ rainy _____ day.

DAY II

Read the passage. Then, answer the questions.

Continents

Earth has seven continents: Africa, Antarctica, Asia, Australia, Europe, North America, and South America. These continents were once a large piece of land. The land split millions of years ago. Large pieces of land drifted apart. The oceans filled the spaces between the pieces of land. The continents we know today are the result. Each continent looks different and has different plants, animals, and weather. North America does not have tigers, but Asia does. Antarctica does not have a jungle, but South America does. The continents are similar in some ways. Some similarities may be because the continents were once one large piece of land.

9. What is the main idea of this passage?

    A. Earth is made of land and water.

    B. Earth has seven continents that were once one piece of land.

    C. Earth has many types of animals, plants, and weather.

10. List the seven continents. _Africa, Antarctica, Asia, Australia, Europe, North America, South America_

11. When did the continents form? _Millions of years ago._

12. What type of land can you find in South America? _Jungles_

13. Why might continents with an ocean between them have similarities? _Both might have lots of animals._

FACTOID: Hummingbirds are the only birds that can hover and fly upside down.

Make one dollar in change five different ways.
EXAMPLE:

quarters	**2**
dimes	**4**
nickels	**2**
pennies	**0**
total	$ **1.00**

1.

quarters	0
dimes	0
nickels	0
pennies	100
total	$ 1.00

2.

quarters	4
dimes	0
nickels	0
pennies	0
total	$ 1.00

3.

quarters	2
dimes	2
nickels	2
pennies	20 no
total	$ 1.00

4.

quarters	0
dimes	10
nickels	0
pennies	0
total	$ 1.00

5.

quarters	2
dimes	0
nickels	0
pennies	50
total	$ 1.00

Circle the adjectives in each sentence.
EXAMPLE:

The (big) (red) wagon rolled down the hill.

6. Justin likes a (soft) pillow.

7. The hikers climbed a (steep) hill.

8. The door made a (screechy) noise.

9. The (hot,) (wet) sand felt good on our feet.

DAY 12

Follow the directions.

10. Color the toucan's beak three different colors.

11. Color the throat and chest orange.

12. Color the feet orange.

13. Color the rest of the toucan black.

14. Draw a branch for the toucan to sit on.

Write about something that you could reuse or recycle. How would you reuse or recycle it?

_____

_____

_____

_____

_____

_____

_____

_____

FITNESS FLASH: Do five push-ups.

* See page ii.

PLACE STICKER HERE

Add or subtract to solve each problem.

1. 28 + 18	2. 23 – 16	3. 46 – 27	4. 34 + 38	5. 77 – 38	6. 49 + 23

7. 35 + 58	8. 85 – 78	9. 48 – 29	10. 49 + 15	11. 96 – 37	12. 68 + 27

13. 47 – 39	14. 37 + 55	15. 71 – 24	16. 57 + 26	17. 92 – 37	18. 64 – 19

Circle the adjectives that describe each underlined noun.

19. I have a blue and purple <u>coat</u>.

20. The little, green <u>snake</u> climbed the tree.

21. Tasha made a dress from colorful, soft <u>cloth</u>.

22. The dark, gray <u>cloud</u> is over my house.

23. I wore my new, brown <u>sandals</u> today.

Read the story. Then, number the events in the order that they happened.

Snowed In

It snowed for three days. When it stopped, the snow was so deep that Ivan and Jacob could not open the cabin door. The men climbed through the upstairs window to get outside. They spent hours shoveling the snow away from the door. At last, they could open the door.

24. _____ The men climbed out the window.

25. _____ It snowed for three days.

26. _____ Ivan and Jacob opened the door.

27. _____ The men shoveled snow for hours.

Quick-Crawling Crab

Have you ever seen a crab crawling on the beach? If you try to move like those fast crustaceans, you can build your upper body, lower body, and core strength.

Sit on the floor. Place your hands behind you and feet in front of you flat on the ground. Use your arms and legs to lift your body off of the ground. Now, crab-walk backward a few yards. Then, crab-walk forward. It is hard to keep your weight off the ground for long!

Once you have mastered the crab-walk, you can make the activity more challenging. Use a stopwatch or timer to see how long you can crab-walk, or increase your speed. Practice the crab-walk throughout the summer, and you will feel your body become stronger.

> **FACTOID:** The Bahamas once had an undersea post office.

* See page ii.

PLACE STICKER HERE

Find the length of each line segment in inches. Round each number to the nearest inch. Write the measurements in the boxes. Then, add the measurements.

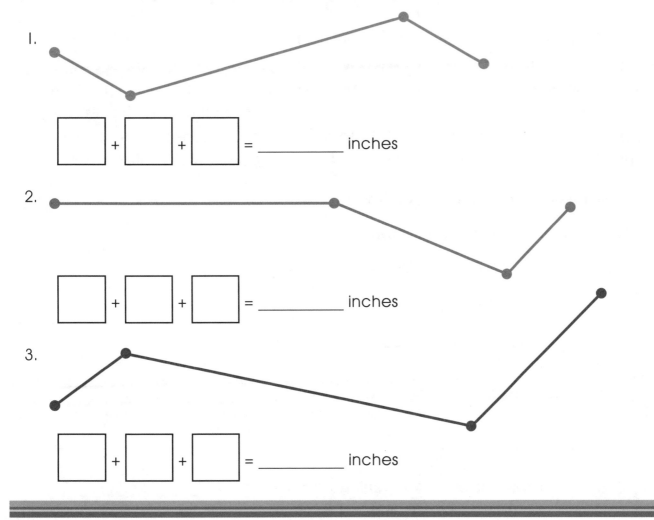

1.

☐ + ☐ + ☐ = _____ inches

2.

☐ + ☐ + ☐ = _____ inches

3.

☐ + ☐ + ☐ = _____ inches

Add the suffixes *-er* and *-est* to each word.
EXAMPLE:

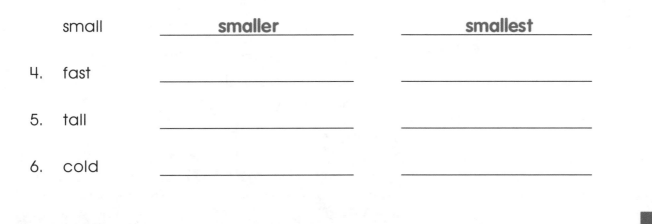

small   **smaller**   **smallest**

4.   fast   _____   _____

5.   tall   _____   _____

6.   cold   _____   _____

DAY 14

Read the passage. Then, answer the questions.

Sleep

Are you ever sleepy in the middle of the day? Children need about 8 to 11 hours of sleep each night. During sleep, your body rests and gets ready for another day. It is important to be rested for school every morning. If you are tired, you might have trouble paying attention to your teacher. If you have a hard time falling asleep, try reading a book instead of watching TV before bedtime. Go to bed at the same time every night. Play soft music to help you get sleepy. Soon, you will be dreaming!

7. What is the main idea of this passage?

   A. Getting enough sleep is important.

   B. Reading a book can help you go to sleep.

   C. You should dream every night.

8. How much sleep do children need? _____

9. What might happen at school if you are tired? _____

   _____

10. What can you do instead of watching TV at bedtime? _____

   _____

11. When should you go to bed?

   A. 10 P.M.

   B. only when you feel sleepy

   C. at the same time every night

FITNESS FLASH: Do 10 lunges.

* See page ii.

PLACE STICKER HERE

Measure the length of each object in centimeters.

1. _____ cm

2. _____ cm

3. _____ cm

4. _____ cm

5. _____ cm

6. _____ cm

Write an adjective to complete each sentence.

7. Gabriel showed me the _____ picture.

8. The _____ puppy is chasing his tail.

9. That _____ bird flies south for the winter.

10. Stephen carried the _____ suitcase.

11. That book with the _____ cover is mine.

Circle the letter next to the main idea of each paragraph.

12. Sometimes I have strange dreams. Once, I dreamed I was floating inside a spaceship. When I woke up, I thought I was still floating. I reminded myself that it was just a dream. When I told my mom about it, she said that she sometimes has strange dreams too.

    A. I dreamed I was floating in space.

    B. My mom had the same dream I did.

    C. Sometimes we have strange dreams.

13. I like to read. In the summer, I go to the library twice a week. I check out books about lemurs and airplanes. I also like to read about rain forests. The librarian helps me find books I will like.

    A. I read books about race cars in the summer.

    B. I find books to read at the library.

    C. Librarians are friendly and helpful.

Read each word. Change the underlined letter or letters to make a new word.
EXAMPLE:

press **mess**   14. take _____   15. well _____

16. those _____   17. dove _____   18. ship _____

19. true _____   20. bud _____   21. fast _____

22. ride _____   23. like _____   24. mist _____

CHARACTER CHECK: Write and illustrate a short story about a character who is honest. Give your story a happy ending. Then, share your story with a family member.

PLACE STICKER HERE

One meter is 100 centimeters. Circle your estimate for each question.

EXAMPLE:

A dictionary is

A.   taller than one meter.

(B.   shorter than one meter.)

1.   A house is

A.   taller than one meter.

B.   shorter than one meter.

2.   A baby is

A.   longer than one meter.

B.   shorter than one meter.

3.   Your front door is

A.   taller than one meter.

B.   shorter than one meter.

4.   A pencil is

A.   longer than one meter.

B.   shorter than one meter.

5.   A paper clip is

A.   longer than one meter.

B.   shorter than one meter.

Write the two words that make each contraction.
EXAMPLE:

hasn't _____**has not**_____

6.   I'm _____

7.   you'll _____

8.   wouldn't _____

9.   we've _____

10.   we'd _____

11.   you're _____

12.   she's _____

13.   isn't _____

14.   I'll _____

DAY 16

Use the table of contents to answer the questions.

15. On which page should you begin reading about where ants live?

_____

16. Which chapter would tell about the different kinds of ants?

_____

17. On which page would you look to find the index?

_____

18. What is the title of the first chapter?

_____

Draw an X over each misspelled word. Write each word correctly.

19. Marcus has a new electrik car.   _____

20. Bonnie takes the fast trane to work.   _____

21. Let's keap together when we go.   _____

22. My dad drives a large dump truk.   _____

23. Let's plae baseball.   _____

FACTOID: Old beds were held up with rope. That's why we say, "Sleep tight."

PLACE STICKER HERE

Circle the object in each row that holds the most.

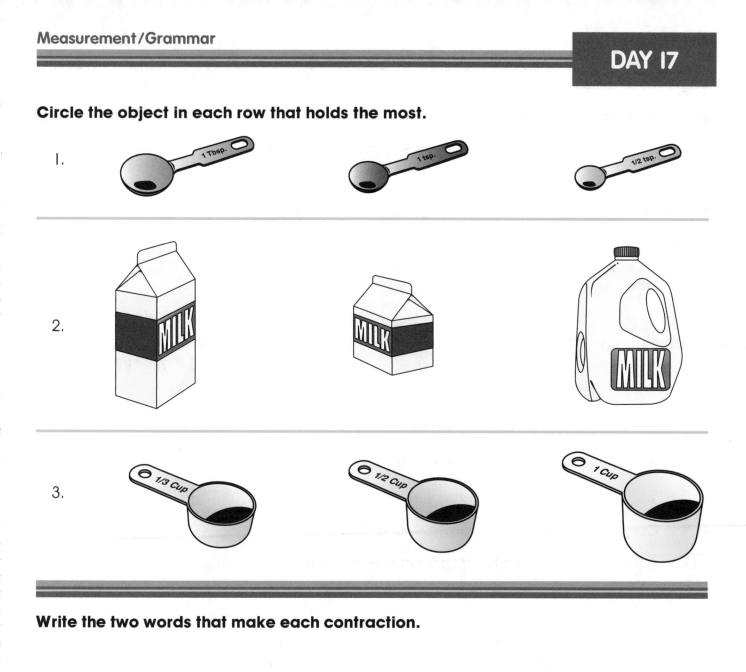

1.

1 Tbsp.   1 tsp.   1/2 tsp.

2.

MILK   MILK   MILK

3.

1/3 Cup   1/2 Cup   1 Cup

Write the two words that make each contraction.

4. she's _____

5. he's _____

6. aren't _____

7. you've _____

8. I've _____

9. I'd _____

10. it's _____

11. haven't _____

12. she'll _____

13. shouldn't _____

14. we'll _____

15. we're _____

DAY 17

Read the passage. Then, answer the questions.

Changing with the Seasons

We change the types of clothes we wear with the seasons to protect us from the weather. Animals do the same when the seasons change.

For example, the arctic fox has a thick, white fur coat in the winter. A white coat is not easy to see in the snow. This helps the fox hide. When spring comes, the fox's fur changes to brown or gray. It becomes the color of the ground.

The ptarmigan bird, or snow chicken, has white feathers in the winter. It, too, is hard to see in the snow. In the spring, the bird **molts**. This means that it sheds all of its feathers. The bird grows new feathers that are gray or brown and speckled. When the bird is very still, it looks like a rock.

16. What is the passage mostly about?

    A. how people change with the seasons

    B. how seasons change

    C. how animals change with the seasons

17. What color is the arctic fox's fur in the winter?

    A. brown   B. white

    C. black   D. gray

18. What happens to the ptarmigan bird in the spring?

    A. It molts.   B. It flies south.

    C. Its feathers turn red.   D. It hides near rocks.

19. What does **molt** mean in the story?

    A. to change colors   B. to shed feathers

    C. to hide from an enemy   D. to run quickly

FITNESS FLASH: Do 10 sit-ups.

* See page ii.

PLACE STICKER HERE

Write the temperature on the first line. Then, write if it is warm or cold.

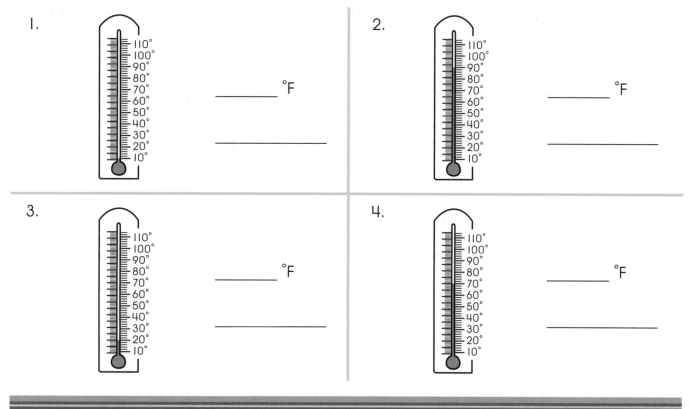

1. _____ °F

    _____

2. _____ °F

    _____

3. _____ °F

    _____

4. _____ °F

    _____

Circle and write the correct contraction to complete each sentence.

EXAMPLE:

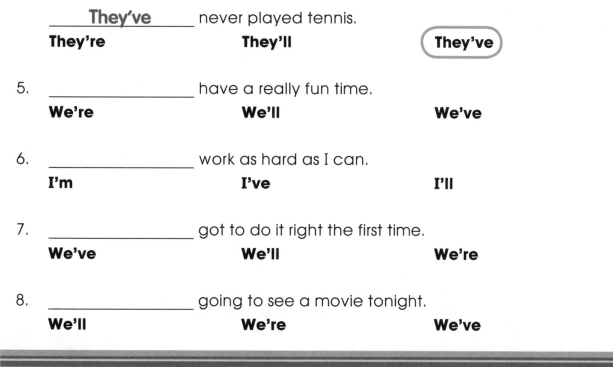

_____They've_____ never played tennis.

They're   **They'll**   (**They've**)

5. _____ have a really fun time.

We're   **We'll**   **We've**

6. _____ work as hard as I can.

I'm   **I've**   **I'll**

7. _____ got to do it right the first time.

We've   **We'll**   **We're**

8. _____ going to see a movie tonight.

We'll   **We're**   **We've**

DAY 18

Read the story about Max and Julia. Write *M* beside the phrases that describe Max, and *J* beside the phrases that describe Julia. Write *B* if the phrase describes both children.

Max and Julia

Max and Julia are twins. They have brown eyes and black hair. They are eight years old and go to school. Julia likes math, and Max likes to read. They both like to play outside. Julia likes to play basketball. Max likes to run and play tag. Julia likes to ride her bike while Max walks their dog, Rover.

9. _____ has brown eyes

10. _____ likes to run

11. _____ is a twin

12. _____ likes to play basketball

13. _____ likes to read

14. _____ likes math

15. _____ is seven

16. _____ has a pet

17. _____ likes to ride bikes

18. _____ has black hair

Write the letter of the correct definition next to each vocabulary word.

19. _____ desert

A.   a tall piece of land

20. _____ mountain

B.   a flowing body of water

21. _____ valley

C.   a body of water surrounded by land

22. _____ ocean

D.   low land between mountains or hills

23. _____ lake

E.   a place that is very dry

24. _____ river

F.   a body of water that surrounds continents.

FACTOID: A group of frogs is called an army.

PLACE
STICKER
HERE

Names of days of the week begin with capital letters. Answer each question with the names of the days.

1. Write the names of the three days that have exactly six letters. _____

   _____

2. Which day comes after Friday? _____

3. Which two days have names with exactly eight letters? _____

   _____

4. _____ has exactly seven letters, and _____ has nine.

To abbreviate a word means to shorten it. Draw a line to match each word to its abbreviation.

5.	December	Dr.		6.	Mister	Rd.
	Doctor	oz.			October	ft.
	Thursday	Dec.			foot	Mr.
	ounce	Jan.			Avenue	Ave.
	January	Thurs.			Road	Oct.

7.	yard	Jr.		8.	Saturday	Sr.
	March	Wed.			Senior	St.
	Junior	yd.			Monday	Mon.
	inch	in.			Fahrenheit	F
	Wednesday	Mar.			Street	Sat.

DAY 19

Write the words from the word bank in alphabetical order.

her	turn	are	more	third	part
card	word	bud	bird	dark	first

9. _____

10. _____

11. _____

12. _____

13. _____

14. _____

15. _____

16. _____

17. _____

18. _____

19. _____

20. _____

Many doors lead to interesting places and things. Think of a door that could lead you to an interesting place. Describe the door and what is behind it. On a separate sheet of paper, draw a picture of your door.

_____

_____

_____

_____

FITNESS FLASH: Do 10 squats.

* See page ii.

PLACE STICKER HERE

Write the name of each shape.

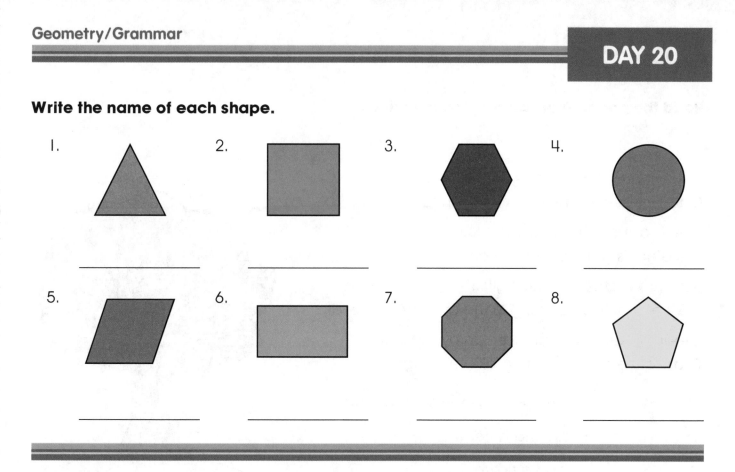

1.

2.

3.

4.

_____

_____

_____

_____

5.

6.

7.

8.

_____

_____

_____

_____

Write _yes_ if the sentence is complete. Write _no_ if it is not complete.

EXAMPLE:

Inside a large. _____no_____

9. Someone is walking on the sidewalk. _____

10. I went to a movie last night. _____

11. Played in the park by. _____

12. What is the? _____

13. Under the swing in front of the house. _____

14. Every Sunday afternoon. _____

15. Did you enjoy reading that book? _____

DAY 20

Read the poem. Then, answer the questions.

Two

Two living things, blowing in the wind.
One stands straight, the other bends.

One is a strong tree growing tall.
The other is grass ever so small.

Both are Mother Nature's gifts.
The tree you can climb. On the grass, you can sit.

Green is their color, brought on by the spring.
Grass or trees, they both make me sing!

16.   What two things is the poem comparing?

    A.   the grass and a tree

    B.   a tree and a flower

    C.   the wind and the rain

17.   Read each description. Decide if the words describe the grass, a tree, or both.
Write an X in each correct column.

	Grass	Tree
living thing		
stands straight in the wind		
bends in the wind		
tall		
small		
can be climbed		
can be sat on		
green in color		

CHARACTER CHECK: Brainstorm a list of positive, encouraging words and phrases. Refer to your list when you begin to feel discouraged with a task.

PLACE
STICKER
HERE

Paper Towel Preserver

Can you dunk a glass with a paper towel inside it into an aquarium filled with water and have the paper towel stay dry?

Materials:

- large, clear container or aquarium
- drinking glass (any size)
- dry paper towel
- water

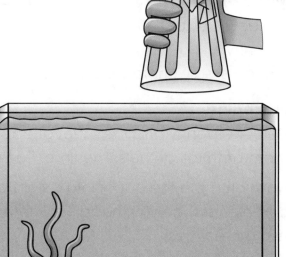

Procedure:

Have an adult help you fill the aquarium with water.

Gently stuff the paper towel into the bottom of the glass. Turn the glass upside down to make sure that the paper towel does not fall out.

Keep the glass upside down. Slowly lower it straight down into the container of water until the paper towel and glass are both completely underwater. (Note: the experiment will not work if you tilt the glass at all.) Remove the glass from the water. Is the paper towel wet or dry?

What's This All About?

This experiment shows that air takes up space. As you lower the glass into the container of water, the air inside the glass displaces, or pushes away, the water in the container. Because the water is displaced, the paper towel stays dry.

More Fun Ideas to Try:

If you are having a hard time seeing how air takes up space, put your hands on your chest. Inhale, hold your breath, and then exhale. Did you feel how air takes up space in your lungs?

BONUS

Air Friction

Which would drop faster if it fell from a two-story building: a penny or sheet of paper? Which would hit the ground first? How does air affect falling objects?

Materials:
- sheet of paper
- penny
- a few small, unbreakable objects

Procedure:

Hold the penny and the sheet of paper in front of you and higher than your head. Let them both fall at the same time. Repeat this activity two more times.

Now, crumple the paper into a tight ball. Hold the paper and the penny in front of you and higher than your head. Let them both fall at the same time. Repeat this activity two more times.

Repeat the experiment with two sheets of paper that are crumpled, one loosely and one tightly. Then, try different coins and other objects. Which object falls the fastest?

What's This All About?

Even though we cannot see air, it has force. By crumpling the paper, you reduced the amount of force the air was able to put on the paper. We call this force *friction*.

Sometimes it is good to have a lot of air friction. For example, a person using a parachute would want friction. The friction created by the parachute would slow her descent to Earth. Sometimes it is good to have less air friction, such as a pilot trying to go fast in an airplane.

More Fun Ideas to Try:
- Make a simple parachute that uses air friction to slow a falling object. Use different materials (paper, fabrics, plastic bags) to make the parachute.
- With an adult, find pictures of different types of cars on the Internet. Look at their designs. Which cars do you think would cause less air friction?

Locate It!

A grid (set of lines on a map) and coordinates (the letters and numbers beside the grid) help you locate places on a map. To find the mall on the map, look at section A,1. Use the map grid and map key to fill in the blanks with the coordinates for each place.

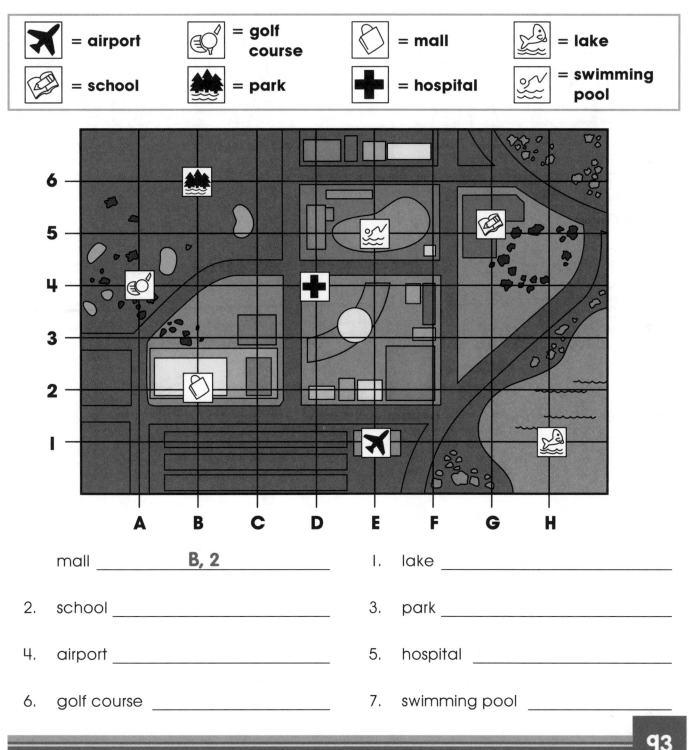

| = airport | = golf course | = mall | = lake |
| = school | = park | = hospital | = swimming pool |

mall ___**B, 2**___

1. lake _____

2. school _____

3. park _____

4. airport _____

5. hospital _____

6. golf course _____

7. swimming pool _____

BONUS

Silver City Championship

Your favorite baseball team is in the championship game. Follow the steps to find out where your friends are sitting at the game.

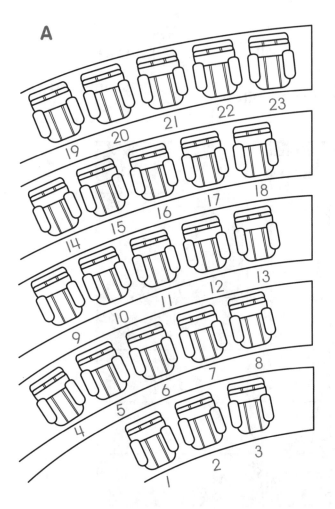

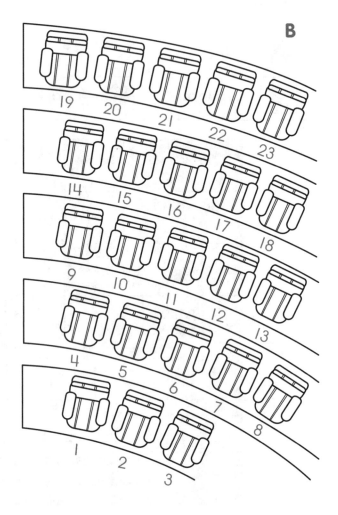

1. Greg is sitting in seat A, 11. Draw a red circle around Greg's seat.

2. Shauna is sitting in seat B, 9. Draw a blue square around Shauna's seat.

3. Craig is sitting in seat B, 5. Draw a green triangle around Craig's seat.

4. Phillip is sitting in seat A, 2. Color Phillip's seat orange.

5. Beth is sitting in seat A, 6. Color Beth's seat purple.

Continent Scramble

A continent is the largest landmass on Earth. There are seven continents in the world. List the seven continents by unscrambling each name. Then, look at the map. Write the letter of each continent next to its name.

1. _____ ACIFRA _____

2. _____ THORN MICAERA _____

3. _____ EPRUEO _____

4. _____ HOUTS RECIMAA _____

5. _____ SAAI _____

6. _____ CTARNATCAI _____

7. _____ STRLAIAUA _____

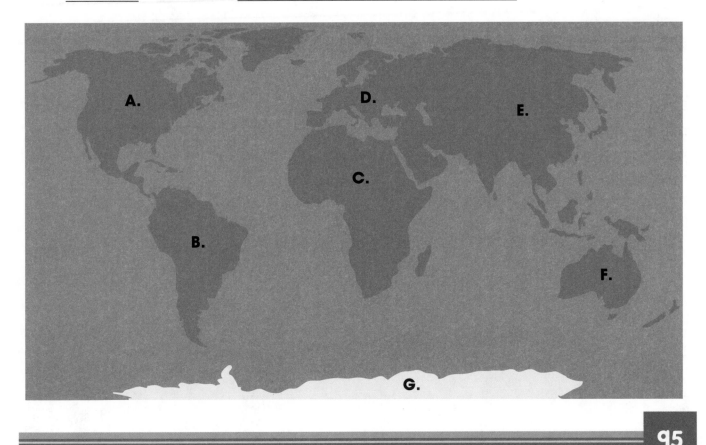

BONUS

Take It Outside!

Go outside with an adult. Take a notebook, a pencil, and a ruler that measures inches and centimeters. Find objects. Measure their lengths. Record each object's length in inches and centimeters. Compare the measurements. Which objects are the shortest, and which are longest?

Play an outdoor observation game with a friend or family member. Find an object that is a three-dimensional geometric shape (sphere, cube, cylinder, cone, prism, or pyramid). Describe the shape to your friend. For example, to describe a beach ball, you would say, "I see a sphere." Take turns describing and identifying shapes.

Go outside with an adult. Take a pencil and a notebook. List some actions that have already happened. Examples include a house that has been built (built), a child who passed by (walked), a man getting out of a car (drove). When you are finished, look at the past-tense verbs on your list. Write a sentence with each verb.

* See page ii.

Monthly Goals

Think of three goals to set for yourself this month. For example, you may want to learn five new math facts each week. Write your goals on the lines and review them with an adult.

Place a sticker next to each goal that you complete. Feel proud that you have met your goals!

1. _____ PLACE STICKER HERE

2. _____ PLACE STICKER HERE

3. _____ PLACE STICKER HERE

Word List

The following words are used in this section. They are good words for you to know. Read each word. Use a dictionary to look up each word that you do not know. Then, write two sentences. Use a word from the word list in each sentence.

channel	medal
election	pilot
festival	schedule
gigantic	sibling
mammal	vote

1. _____

_____

2. _____

_____

Introduction to Endurance

This section includes fitness and character development activities that focus on endurance. These activities are designed to get you moving and thinking about improving your physical fitness and your character.

Physical Endurance

What do playing tag, jumping rope, and riding your bike have in common? They are all great ways to build your endurance!

Having endurance means being able to do an activity for a long time before your body is tired. Your heart is stronger when you have endurance. Your muscles receive more oxygen.

Use the warm summer mornings and sunny days to go outside. Pick activities that you enjoy. Invite a family member on a walk or a bike ride. Play a game of basketball with friends. Leave the less active times for when it is dark, too hot, or raining.

Set an endurance goal this summer. For example, you might jump rope every day until you can jump for two minutes without stopping. Set new goals when you meet your old ones. Be proud of your endurance success!

Endurance and Character Development

Showing mental endurance means sticking with something. You can show mental endurance every day. Staying with a task when you might want to quit and trying your best until it is done are ways that you can show mental endurance.

Build your mental endurance this summer. Think of a time when you were frustrated or bored. Maybe you wanted to take swimming lessons. But, after a few early morning lessons, you were not having as much fun as you imagined. Think about some key points, such as how you asked all spring to take lessons. Be positive. Remind yourself that you have taken only a few lessons. You might get used to the early morning practices. Think of ways to make the lessons more enjoyable, such as sleeping a few extra minutes during the morning car ride. Quitting should be the last resort.

Build your mental endurance now. It will help prepare you for challenges that you may face later!

Circle the shape in each row that represents the bottom face of the solid figure.

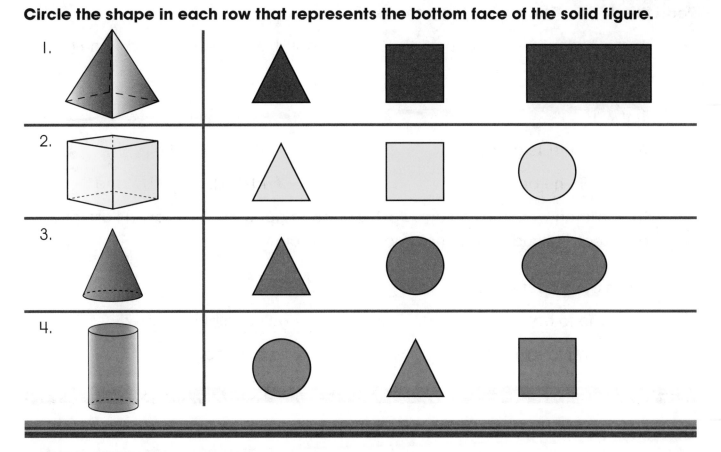

Circle the sentence in each pair that makes sense.

5.   The ice is in the glass.   The glass is in the ice.

6.   Put the porch on the plant.   Put the plant on the porch.

7.   The desk is on the lamp.   The lamp is on the desk.

8.   Please answer the phone.   Answer phone the please.

9.   I will dog the walk.   I will walk the dog.

10. Lawn is good for the rain.   Rain is good for the lawn.

11. Did you see my keys?   Did my keys see you?

12. The piano plays Hugo.   Hugo plays the piano.

Read the stories. Circle what happens next.

13. Jeff put his arms around the box. He could not lift it. He would need some help. The box was too heavy for him.

    Jeff will _____ .

    A. run outside and play   B. ask his dad for help

    C. sit on the box   D. send the box to his friend

14. The children were playing outside. It started to get dark. They saw a flash of light and heard a loud sound. The wind began to blow.

    "Let's go," shouted Hunter. "It's _____."

    A. time to eat   B. going to blow us away

    C. going to rain soon   D. time for bed

Write each word from the word bank under the correct heading.

ball	beans	blocks	bread	cheese	corn
doll	fox	horse	kite	monkey	tiger

Animals	**Toys**	**Food**
_____	_____	_____
_____	_____	_____
_____	_____	_____
_____	_____	_____

FACTOID: The amount of water pouring over Niagara Falls each second could fill 13,000 bathtubs.

PLACE STICKER HERE

Look at each solid figure. Each side is called a face. Write the number of faces for each solid.

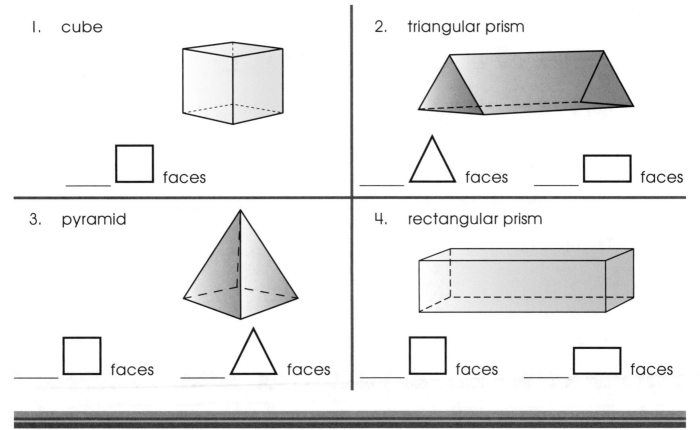

1. cube

_____ faces

2. triangular prism

_____ faces   _____ faces

3. pyramid

_____ faces   _____ faces

4. rectangular prism

_____ faces   _____ faces

A declarative sentence makes a statement. Write _D_ for each declarative sentence. Write _ND_ for each sentence that is not declarative.

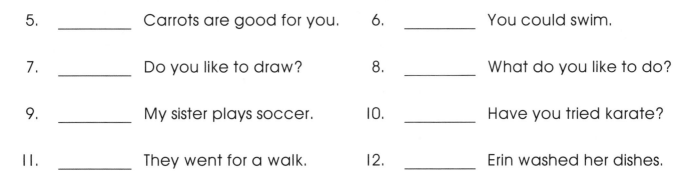

5. _____ Carrots are good for you.

6. _____ You could swim.

7. _____ Do you like to draw?

8. _____ What do you like to do?

9. _____ My sister plays soccer.

10. _____ Have you tried karate?

11. _____ They went for a walk.

12. _____ Erin washed her dishes.

DAY 2

Write the words in each sentence in alphabetical order. Begin each sentence with a capital letter. The first one has been done for you.

EXAMPLE:

talk did she with you? **Did she talk with you?**

13. I notebook there left my. _____

14. grapes ate Anna four. _____

15. wildflowers the Isabelle smelled. _____

16. turtles snapping I like. _____

17. donkeys do hay eat? _____

18. water careful in be the. _____

Imagine that you are collecting items for a time capsule that will be opened in 20 years. What things would you put in the capsule to tell about your life right now?

_____

_____

_____

_____

_____

FITNESS FLASH: Do 10 jumping jacks.

* See page ii.

PLACE STICKER HERE

Add or subtract to solve each problem.

1. 24
    + 12

2. 34
    + 23

3. 11
    + 46

4. 21
    + 67

5. 53
    + 16

6. 75
    − 11

7. 87
    − 24

8. 67
    − 33

9. 57
    − 32

10. 34
    − 12

11. 43
    + 28

12. 56
    + 27

13. 62
    + 19

14. 27
    + 37

15. 49
    + 24

An interrogative sentence asks a question. Write *I* for each interrogative sentence. Write *D* for each declarative sentence.

16. _____ What time will we eat?

17. _____ I have a sandwich.

18. _____ Grant ate a pickle.

19. _____ Do you smell the pie?

20. _____ Who ate an orange?

21. _____ What kind of drink is this?

22. _____ I ate with my friends.

23. _____ Ian cleaned his room.

Read the TV schedule. Then, answer the questions.

Channel		Time							
		7:00	7:30	8:00	8:30	9:00	9:30	10:00	10:30
	2	*Quiz Game Show*	*Jump Start*		*Summer the Dog*			News	
	4	*Lucky Guess*	*You Should Know*	Wednesday Night at the Movies *Friends Forever*				News	
	5	*Best Friends*	*Mary's Secret*	*Where They Are*	*Time to Hope*	*Tom's Talk Show*		News	
	7	*123 Oak Street*	*Lost Alone*	*One More Time*	Sports			News	
	11	*Your Health*	*Eating Right*	*Food News*		*Cooking With Kate*		*Home Decor*	*Shop Now*
	24	*Silly Rabbit*	*Clyde the Clown*	*Ball o' Fun*	*Slime and Rhyme*	*Cartoon Alley*		*Fun Times*	*Make Me Laugh*

24. What does this schedule show?
    - A. times and channels of TV shows
    - B. times and channels of radio programs
    - C. the number of people who like different shows

25. On which channels is the news on at 10:00?
    - A. 2, 5, and 11
    - B. 3, 4, and 11
    - C. 2, 4, 5, and 7

26. What time does the show *Silly Rabbit* begin?
    - A. 7:00
    - B. 7:30
    - C. 8:30

FACTOID: Camels have three sets of eyelids to protect their eyes from sand.

PLACE STICKER HERE

Write the letter of the button that answers each riddle.

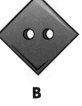

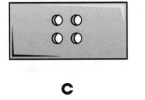

A   **B**   **C**   **D**

1. I do not have corners. I have 4 lines of symmetry. Which button am I?

2. I am not round. I have more than 4 corners. I have 1 line of symmetry. Which button am I?

3. I have 4 corners. I have 2 lines of symmetry. My sides are not all equal in length. Which button am I?

4. On a separate sheet of paper, write a riddle for the remaining button. Ask a family member to guess which button you described.

Change each declarative sentence into an interrogative sentence.
EXAMPLE:

The busy mail carrier is leaving.   **Is the busy mail carrier leaving?**

5. That man is Gary's father. _____

6. She can ride her new bike. _____

7. I will ride the black horse. _____

DAY 4

In a dictionary, guide words are at the top of each page. The guide word on the left tells the first word on the page. The guide word on the right tells the last word on the page. Circle the word that would be on the page with each set of guide words.

8. **patter — penguin**

   panda   pit   paw

9. **match — monkey**

   math   magic   motor

10. **bear — buffalo**

    bunny   bat   bison

11. **hammer — happy**

    hall   hand   hair

12. **rabbit — rack**

    race   racket   radio

Run for Fun and Endurance

Running is a great way to improve your endurance. Put on some comfortable running shoes and stretch for a few minutes. Whether you run in place, in the yard, or at the park, time how long you run. Repeat these runs a few times each week. After each run, record how long you ran. Try to increase the time slightly every week. By the end of the summer, you will be able to run longer and will have increased your endurance.

FITNESS FLASH: Jog in place for 30 seconds.

* See page ii.

PLACE STICKER HERE

Draw the other half of the picture so that both halves are the same.

An exclamatory sentence shows strong emotions or feelings. Write _E_ for each exclamatory sentence. Write _D_ for each declarative sentence. Write _I_ for each interrogative sentence.

1. _____ What did they say?

2. _____ I am so happy for you!

3. _____ It's a boy!

4. _____ That is wonderful news!

5. _____ The card is green.

6. _____ Can I borrow a pencil?

Write each exclamatory sentence with a capital letter and an exclamation point (!).

7. watch out _____

8. i had a great day _____

DAY 5

Read the story. Then, complete the picture to match the story.

Margaret planted five flowers in pots. They grew fast. She put the flowers in a row. The white flower was in the middle. The purple flower was second. The orange flower was not first. The yellow flower was last. Where was the pink flower? Where does the orange flower go?

Make as many new words as you can using the letters in each word below.

9. chart

10. start

11. craft

_____

_____

_____

_____

_____

_____

_____

_____

_____

_____

_____

_____

_____

_____

_____

CHARACTER CHECK: Brainstorm some obstacles you might encounter while trying to achieve your goals this summer. Write one way to overcome each obstacle.

PLACE STICKER HERE

Multiply to find each product. Then, draw a line to match each set to the correct multiplication problem.

EXAMPLE:

$4 \times 3 =$ **12**

1. $3 \times 3 =$ _____

2. $5 \times 2 =$ _____

3. $3 \times 2 =$ _____

4. $2 \times 4 =$ _____

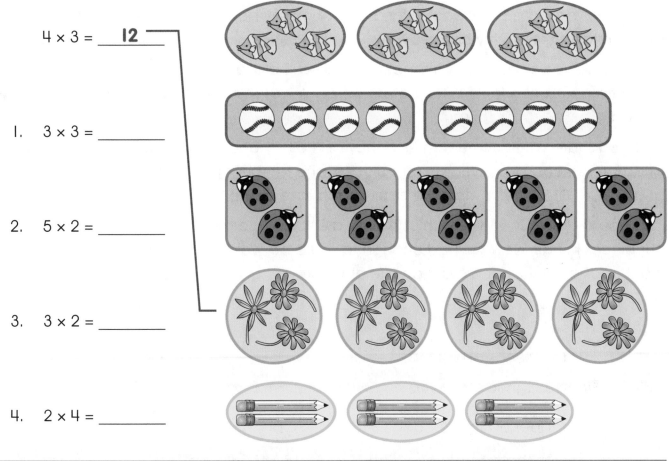

An imperative sentence gives a command. Write **IM** for each imperative sentence. Write **D** for each declarative sentence. Write **I** for each interrogative sentence. Write **E** for each exclamatory sentence.

5. _____ Make a card for Mom.

6. _____ Use markers.

7. _____ She will love it!

8. _____ Show your mom.

9. _____ Tell her how you made it.

10. _____ Cards are great gifts.

11. _____ Has your dad seen it?

12. _____ The card looks great!

DAY 6

Read the story. Then, answer the questions.

The Giant Cookie

My mother baked a giant cookie for me. I sat on my porch to eat it. But, before I could take a bite, my friend Ivy came by.

"Will you share your cookie with me?" Ivy asked. I broke my cookie into two pieces: one for me and one for Ivy. But, before we could each take a bite, Jermaine and Drew came by.

"Will you share your cookie with us?" they asked. Ivy and I each broke our cookie into two more pieces. Now, we had four pieces: one for me, one for Ivy, one for Jermaine, and one for Drew. But, before we could each take a bite, four more friends came by.

"Will you share your cookie with us?" they asked. Ivy, Jermaine, Drew, and I all broke our pieces in half. Now we had enough to share between eight friends. I looked at my giant cookie. It was not a giant cookie anymore.

"Hey, does anyone know what is gigantic when there's one but small when there are eight?" I asked.

"No, what?" my friends asked.

"My cookie!" I laughed.

13. What happened to the cookie?

    A. It was shared between friends.   B. It was lost.

    C. It ran away.   D. It was dropped on the floor.

14. Number the events from the story in order.

    _____ Jermaine and Drew came by.

    _____ Mother baked a cookie.

    _____ Ivy came by.

    _____ Four friends came by.

FACTOID: Every ton of recycled paper saves about 24 trees.

PLACE
STICKER
HERE

Multiply to find each product.

1. 5 × 1 = _____

2. 5 × 5 = _____

3. 3 × 4 = _____

4. 1 × 0 = _____

5. 2 × 2 = _____

6. 4 × 5 = _____

7. 3 × 5 = _____

8. 1 × 1 = _____

9. 2 × 5 = _____

10.   7
    × 1

11.   4
    × 2

12.   2
    × 3

13.   3
    × 3

14.   4
    × 0

Write two exclamatory sentences and two declarative sentences. Use a word from the word bank in each sentence.

attention	calmly	famous	free	million
moment	rain	shiver	station	strange

15. _____

16. _____

17. _____

18. _____

DAY 7

Use the dictionary entry to answer the questions.

> **germ** \\'jerm\ *n* **I.** disease-producing microbe **2.** a bud or seed

19. What part of speech is germ? _____

20. Which definition of germ deals with growing plants? _____

21. Would germinate come before or after germ in the dictionary? _____

22. Use germ in a sentence. _____

_____

Write a title for each list.

23. _____
robin
wren
blue jay
canary

24. _____
paper
glue
scissors
crayons

25. _____
lion
tiger
bear
elephant

26. _____
milk
tea
water
juice

FITNESS FLASH: Hop on your right foot for 30 seconds.

* See page ii.

PLACE
STICKER
HERE

Solve each problem.

1. Maddie has 3 vases with 4 flowers in each vase. How many total flowers does she have?

    _____ × _____ = _____ flowers

2. Mario has 4 packs of gum. There are 5 pieces in each pack. How many pieces of gum does he have?

    _____ × _____ = _____ pieces

3. Jawan has 3 glasses. He put 2 straws in each glass. How many straws did Jawan put in the glasses?

    _____ × _____ = _____ straws

4. We have 4 tables for the party. Each table needs 4 chairs. How many total chairs do we need?

    _____ × _____ = _____ chairs

Read each sentence. Then, write a period (.), a question mark (?), or an exclamation point (!) at the end of each sentence.

5. Soon, we will visit Uncle Ben and Aunt Cathy _____

6. Will Jeremy ride his bike to school this year _____

7. That is great news _____

8. Did you have fun at Lola's party _____

9. My family went on a camping trip _____

10. Have you gone hiking before _____

11. Watch out for that bee _____

DAY 8

Read the paragraph. Then, answer the questions.

Megan's Day

Megan got up late today, so she missed the bus. Her mother had to walk Megan to school. She was tired and cranky when she got there. She promised herself that she would never sleep late again.

12.   Why did Megan miss the bus? _____

13.   Why did she have to walk? _____

_____

14.   What advice do you have for Megan? _____

_____

Imagine that when you go to your mailbox one day, you find a treasure map with a letter addressed to you. Write a story about the letter and map. Who sent the letter? If you look for the treasure, do you find it? If you find it, what is it?

_____

_____

_____

_____

_____

FACTOID: Deserts cover 25% of Earth's surface.

PLACE STICKER HERE

Divide each set of objects into 2 equal groups. Then, divide to find each quotient.

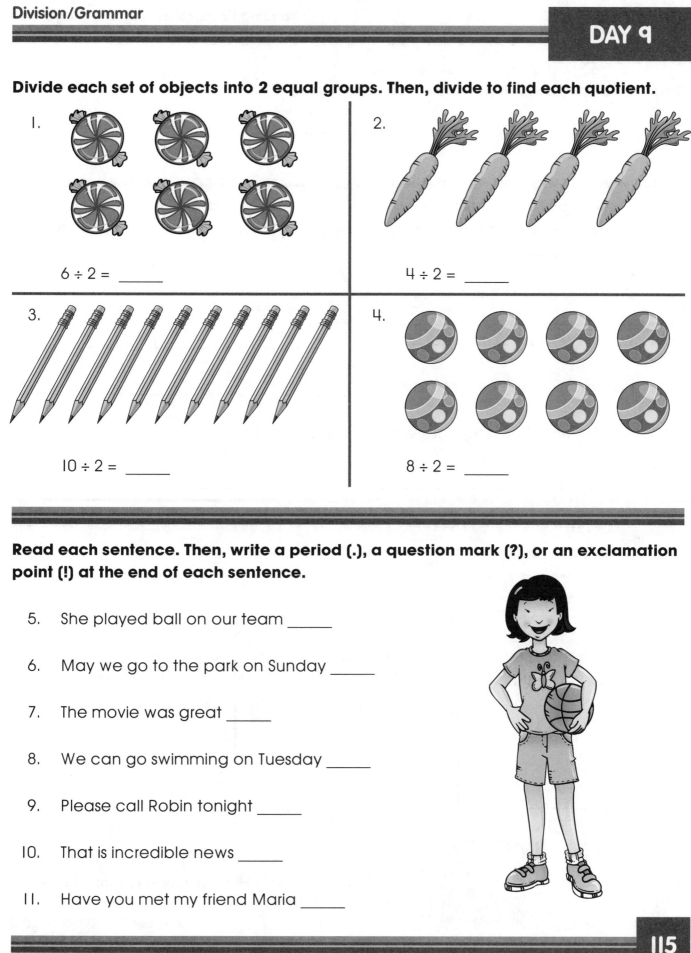

1. $6 \div 2 =$ _____

2. $4 \div 2 =$ _____

3. $10 \div 2 =$ _____

4. $8 \div 2 =$ _____

Read each sentence. Then, write a period (.), a question mark (?), or an exclamation point (!) at the end of each sentence.

5.   She played ball on our team _____

6.   May we go to the park on Sunday _____

7.   The movie was great _____

8.   We can go swimming on Tuesday _____

9.   Please call Robin tonight _____

10. That is incredible news _____

11. Have you met my friend Maria _____

DAY 9

Read the paragraph. Then, follow the directions.

Lauren's Summer

Lauren is very busy in the summer. She likes to sleep until eight o'clock. After she gets up, she helps her father work in the garden. Lauren reads and plays with her friends every day. She also likes to swim and play soccer with her brothers. Most of all, she likes to ride her bike.

12.   Underline the topic sentence.

13.   What time does Lauren get up? _____

14.   How does Lauren help her father? _____

15.   Write three other things that Lauren likes to do in the summer. _____

_____

Write a word from the word bank to answer each riddle.

clock	donkey	table

16.   What has four legs but never walks anywhere?

a _____

17.   What has two hands but does not clap?

a _____

18.   What kind of key has four legs and a tail?

a _____

FITNESS FLASH: Hop on your left foot 10 times.

* See page ii.

PLACE STICKER HERE

Divide each set of objects into 3 equal groups. Then, divide to find each quotient.

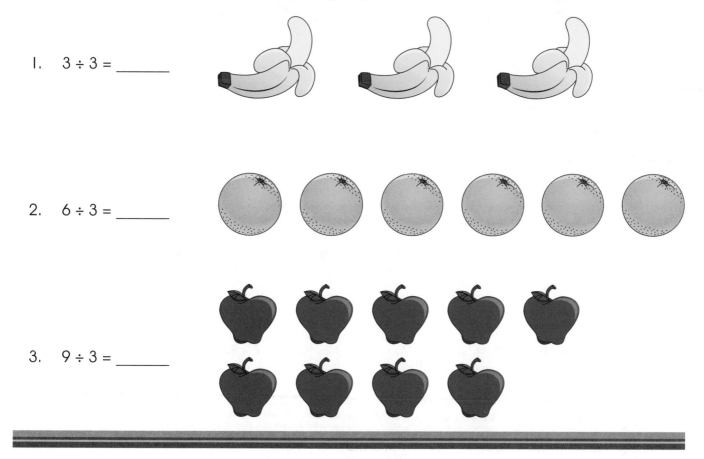

1. $3 \div 3 =$ _____

2. $6 \div 3 =$ _____

3. $9 \div 3 =$ _____

Capitalize the first, last, and all important words in a story or book title. Write each story title correctly.

EXAMPLE:

an exciting camping trip _____ **An Exciting Camping Trip** _____

4. my ride on a donkey _____

5. the day I missed school _____

6. fun, fabulous pets _____

7. a fire drill _____

8. my summer job _____

DAY 10

A thesaurus includes synonyms of words. You can use a thesaurus to make your writing more interesting. Look at this page from a thesaurus. Then, answer the questions.

sad (adj): cheerless, dejected, depressed, dismal, down, forlorn, gloomy, glum, miserable, morose, unhappy	**said** (v): bellowed, echoed, hammered, harped, mentioned, repeated, sang, shouted, spoke, told, whined, whispered, yelled

9. Are the synonyms for the entry words in alphabetical order?_____

10. What does the (adj) after the word sad tell you about the word?

    _____

11. Rewrite this sentence using a synonym for the word sad: The boy was feeling sad

    because he let go of his balloon._____

    _____

Circle and write the correct word to complete each sentence.

12. We dressed in special_____ for the party.
    cloth   **clothes**   **clothed**

13. She turned on the _____ as we came into the room.
    light   **lighted**   **lighting**

14. We like to play in the _____ .
    rain   **rained**   **raining**

CHARACTER CHECK: What is the hardest part about standing up for your beliefs?

PLACE STICKER HERE

Divide to find each quotient.

1. $6\overline{)36}$

2. $7\overline{)42}$

3. $8\overline{)56}$

4. $5\overline{)45}$

5. $3\overline{)21}$

6. $9\overline{)63}$

7. $4\overline{)36}$

8. $6\overline{)54}$

9. $5\overline{)35}$

10. $3\overline{)27}$

11. $2\overline{)18}$

12. $7\overline{)49}$

Read the story. Then, circle each word that should have a capital letter.

Our Camping Trip

mom, dad, and I went camping last week. We went with Uncle seth and Aunt kay. We

had fun. Dad and uncle seth climbed on rocks. Aunt kay and I saw a chipmunk. We

all hiked on exciting trails. There was only one problem. mom, dad, and i did not bring

sweaters. Dad said that it would be warm in the desert. He was wrong. At night, it was

very cold. uncle Seth and aunt kay had sweaters. Mom, dad, and I stayed close to the

fire. Next time, we will bring warmer clothes.

DAY 11

Read each sentence. Then, circle whether each sentence is reality or fantasy.

13. A beaver is a mammal that builds dams.
     reality   **fantasy**

14. The fairy lived inside a mushroom.
     reality   **fantasy**

15. People can build brick walls.
     reality   **fantasy**

16. The dog sang a song.
     reality   **fantasy**

Use the words from the word bank to label the parts of the plant.

bud	flower	leaf	seed	stem	root

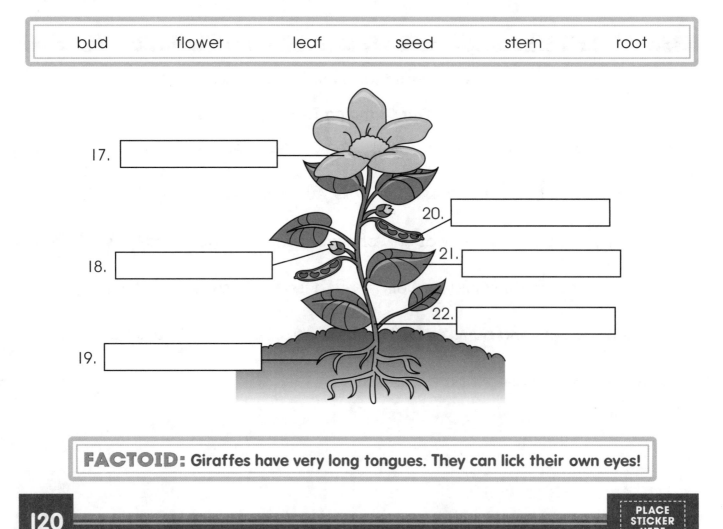

17.

18.

19.

20.

21.

22.

FACTOID: Giraffes have very long tongues. They can lick their own eyes!

PLACE STICKER HERE

Continue each number pattern on the lines. Then, write each rule.

1. 1, 2, 3, 4, _____ , _____ , _____ , _____ , _____ , _____

    Rule: _____

2. 20, 18, 16, 14, _____ , _____ , _____ , _____ , _____ , _____

    Rule: _____

3. 10, 20, 30, 40, _____ , _____ , _____ , _____ , _____ , _____

    Rule: _____

4. 5, 10, 15, 20, _____ , _____ , _____ , _____ , _____ , _____

    Rule: _____

5. 30, 27, 24, 21, _____ , _____ , _____ , _____ , _____ , _____

    Rule: _____

Circle each word that should have a capital letter. Write a period (.) or question mark (?) at the end of each sentence.

6. Reid lives in dallas, texas_____

7. mr. javaris is my neighbor_____

8. is caleb's birthday in april_____

9. my mother and i shop at smith's market_____

10. what is your favorite month of the year_____

Read the passage. Then, answer the questions.

Amelia Earhart

Amelia Earhart was a famous airplane pilot. She was born in 1897. She saw her first airplane at the Iowa State Fair at age 10. Amelia Earhart started taking flying lessons in 1921. Then, she bought her first plane. She named the plane *Canary* because it was bright yellow.

In 1932, Amelia Earhart became the first woman to fly alone across the Atlantic Ocean. The U.S. Congress gave her a medal called the Distinguished Flying Cross after this accomplishment. Amelia Earhart set many new flying records. Also in 1932, she became the first woman to fly alone nonstop from one coast of the United States to another. In 1937, she decided to fly around the world. Her plane was lost over the Pacific Ocean. Amelia Earhart was never heard from again.

11. What is the main idea of this passage?

    A.   Amelia Earhart flew around the world.

    B.   Amelia Earhart was a famous pilot who set many flying records.

    C.   Amelia Earhart had a yellow airplane called *Canary*.

12. Where did Earhart see her first airplane? _____

13. Why did Earhart call her first airplane *Canary*? _____

14. Why did Earhart receive a medal? _____

    _____

15. What happened to Earhart in 1937? _____

    _____

FITNESS FLASH: Do 10 jumping jacks.

* See page ii.

PLACE STICKER HERE

Write the number that the symbol represents in each equation.

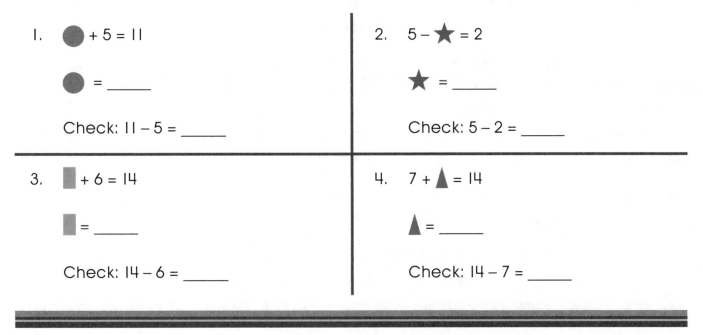

1. ● + 5 = 11

   ● = _____

   Check: 11 – 5 = _____

2. 5 – ★ = 2

   ★ = _____

   Check: 5 – 2 = _____

3. ■ + 6 = 14

   ■ = _____

   Check: 14 – 6 = _____

4. 7 + ▲ = 14

   ▲ = _____

   Check: 14 – 7 = _____

Unscramble and rewrite each sentence correctly. Add capital letters where they are needed. Write a period (.) or question mark (?) at the end of each sentence.

5. birds do live where _____

6. very my hard works sister _____

7. swim can like fish a she _____

8. green grass why is _____

9. water fish in live _____

10. park the go can when we to _____

11. the did go she to store why _____

12. is what name his _____

13. love to i play basketball _____

DAY 13

Read the story. Then, circle the letter of the best summary.

Water Fun

Larry loved to play in the water. Every time it rained, he would run outside to play in the puddles. His dog splashed in the water with him. Larry splashed water on anyone who came near. Soon, his friends would not play with him because he always got them wet. One day, a big truck went by and splashed water all over Larry. He got so wet that he decided not to splash people anymore.

14. A.   Larry liked to play in puddles of water. He got wet. He did not splash anymore.

     B.   Larry liked to play in puddles of water. He splashed water on people. One day a truck splashed him. He stopped splashing others.

A Life Lesson

To persevere means to keep trying even when something is hard to do. Think of a time when you showed perseverance, such as when you learned to ride a bike. Try to remember how hard it was to learn but how exciting it was to reach your goal.

Take time to help a younger sibling or neighbor acquire a new skill. Explain the meaning of perseverance if he gets frustrated. Talk about how hard it was for you to learn a skill when you were younger. You can also share the goals you have now. Celebrate his success when he reaches his goal. Feel proud that you helped him persevere!

FACTOID: Peregrine falcons live on every continent except Antarctica.

PLACE STICKER HERE

Circle the fraction that shows the shaded part of each shape.

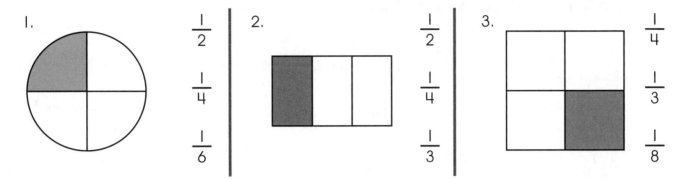

1. $\frac{1}{2}$ $\frac{1}{4}$ $\frac{1}{6}$

2. $\frac{1}{2}$ $\frac{1}{4}$ $\frac{1}{3}$

3. $\frac{1}{4}$ $\frac{1}{3}$ $\frac{1}{8}$

Write the fraction that shows the shaded part of each shape.

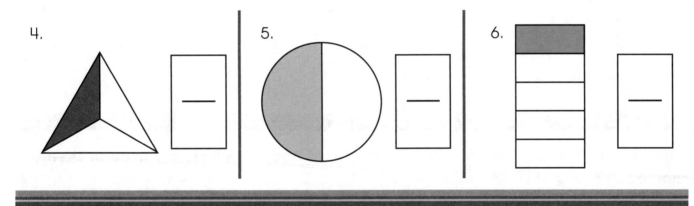

4.

5.

6.

Circle the letter of each correct answer.

7.   Which sentence names three things?

   A.   Casey took a book, a bag, and an umbrella to school.

   B.   Casey took a book bag and an umbrella to school.

8.   Which sentence names two things?

   A.   Wyatt put the lunch, box, and book on the table.

   B.   Wyatt put the lunch box and book on the table.

Look at the index from a book about flowers. Then, write the page number where you would find the information on each flower.

9. tulip _____

10. pansy _____

11. daisy _____

12. rose _____

13. zinnia _____

14. lily _____

A	G	R
allium.......... 45	gardens.........2	rose 21
aster............ 62	gladiolus 7	S
B	I	stamen 6, 7
blossoms 13	iris 8	stigma....... 6, 7
buttercup 65	L	T
C	larkspur........47	thistle 27
cowslip 25	lily 42	tulip 26
D	M	W
daffodil........27	marigold 29	wisteria 20
dahlia 19	P	Z
daisy 15	pansy...........31	zinnia 60
	petals...........6	

Ask an adult to read one word from each group. Circle each word you hear. Then, read each group of words aloud.

15. course	16. floor	17. instead	18. east	19. begin
corner	fix	inside	else	behind
cost	fire	into	easy	began
cook	five	income	engine	before

20. point	21. until	22. throw	23. alarm	24. weather
plane	unusual	through	adjust	wagon
pickle	unlace	those	alone	weave
push	unit	that	afraid	weep

FITNESS FLASH: Jog in place for 30 seconds.

* See page ii.

PLACE STICKER HERE

Draw a line to match the shapes in each group that show the same fraction shaded.

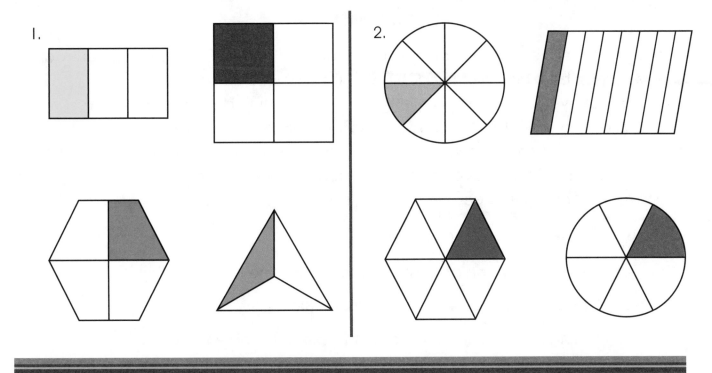

Circle the letter next to each correct answer.

3. Which sentence names five things?

    A.   Tia got an apple, a cupcake, an orange, a carrot, and milk for lunch.

    B.   Tia got an apple cupcake, an orange, a carrot, and milk for lunch.

4. Which sentence names three people?

    A.   Alex Lee, Mason, and Spencer were playing ball.

    B.   Alex, Lee, Mason, and Spencer were playing ball.

Read the passage. Then, answer the questions.

The Right to Vote

Voting in government elections is very important. In the United States and Canada, a person must be a citizen of the country and be at least 18 years old to vote in an election. Not everyone could vote in the past. In the United States, women were not allowed to vote until 1920. A law was passed in 1965 that gave adults of all races the right to vote. When a person votes, he or she helps decide who will serve in the government and what kinds of laws will be passed. Some people say that voting is the most important thing that people can do as citizens.

5.   What is the main idea of this passage?

   A.   A person must be at least 18 years old to vote in an election.

   B.   Not everyone can vote in the United States.

   C.   Voting is an important thing for people to be able to do.

6.   Who can vote in the United States and Canada? _____

_____

7.   When were U.S. women first allowed to vote? _____

8.   What happened in the United States after a law was passed in 1965?

_____

9.   Why is voting important? _____

_____

CHARACTER CHECK: On another sheet of paper, explain why it is important to always try your best.

Color the objects to show each fraction.

EXAMPLE:

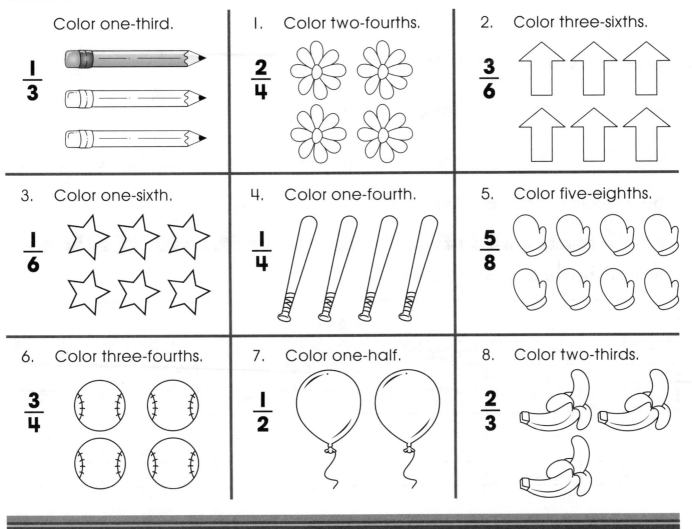

Color one-third.

$\dfrac{1}{3}$

1. Color two-fourths.

$\dfrac{2}{4}$

2. Color three-sixths.

$\dfrac{3}{6}$

3. Color one-sixth.

$\dfrac{1}{6}$

4. Color one-fourth.

$\dfrac{1}{4}$

5. Color five-eighths.

$\dfrac{5}{8}$

6. Color three-fourths.

$\dfrac{3}{4}$

7. Color one-half.

$\dfrac{1}{2}$

8. Color two-thirds.

$\dfrac{2}{3}$

Add commas where they are needed in the paragraph.

Land Formations and Bodies of Water

The earth has many mountains, rivers, lakes oceans and continents. The Andes the

Rockies and the Urals are mountain ranges. The Amazon the Nile and the Hudson are

rivers. Lake Erie Lake Ontario and Lake Huron are three of the Great Lakes. The Pacific

the Atlantic and the Arctic are oceans. Europe, Asia and Africa are continents. New

Zealand Greenland and Iceland are islands.

DAY 16

Write the name of the person who is talking in each sentence.

9. Travis said, "Trent, you need to go to bed." _____

10. "Is this your book, Lamar?" asked Keisha. _____

11. Lamar replied, "No, Keisha, it is not my book." _____

12. "Will you take the dog for a walk, Mia?" asked Mrs. Travers. _____

13. "Would you please go to the store for me?" Sadaf asked. _____

Use the calendar to answer the questions.

August						
Sunday	**Monday**	**Tuesday**	**Wednesday**	**Thursday**	**Friday**	**Saturday**
		1	2	3	4	5
6	7	8	9	10	11	12
13	14	15	16	17	18	19
20	21	22	23	24	25	26
27	28	29	30	31		

14. What day of the week is August 18? _____

15. How many Wednesdays are in August? _____

16. What is the date of the last Saturday in August? _____

17. What day of the week will September 1 be? _____

FACTOID: A rhinoceros's horn isn't really a horn. It's made of tightly pressed hair.

130

PLACE STICKER HERE

Look at the spinner. Then, answer the questions.

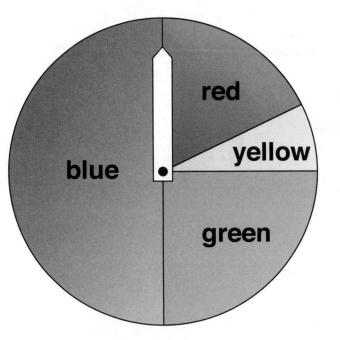

1. Which color will the spinner probably land on most often?

   _____

2. Which color will the spinner probably land on least often?

   _____

3. Do you think the spinner would land on red or green more often?

   _____

4. Do you think the spinner would land on green or yellow more often?

   _____

Rewrite each sentence correctly. Add capital letters, periods, and question marks where they are needed.

5. bobby has a dog named shadow

   _____

6. do bluebirds eat insects

   _____

7. can i borrow your video game

   _____

8. my name is nikki _____

DAY 17

An analogy compares two pairs of items based on a similar relationship between the items. Write the correct word from the word bank to complete each analogy.

| cat | ground | window | ~~water~~ | trees | cow |

EXAMPLE:

Car is to road as boat is to _____**water**_____ .

9. Bird is to sky as worm is to _____ .

10. City is to buildings as forest is to_____ .

11. Knob is to door as pane is to _____ .

12. Cub is to bear as calf is to_____ .

13. Quack is to duck as meow is to_____ .

Fitness Festival

Invite a few friends or family members to a fitness festival. Set up three exercise stations for endurance activities. These could include jumping rope, running in place, hopping on one foot, or doing jumping jacks. Take turns rotating through each station. Rest after each exercise and sip some water. Complete each station twice. After everyone has completed the fitness activities, celebrate together with a healthy snack.

FITNESS FLASH: Hop on your left foot 10 times.

* See page ii.

132

PLACE STICKER HERE

The bar graph shows concession stand sales at a baseball game. Use the bar graph to answer the questions.

1. Which two items had the fewest sales?

   _____

2. Which item had the most sales?

   _____

3. How many more nachos were sold

   than hot dogs? _____

4. How many more chips were sold

   than pretzels? _____

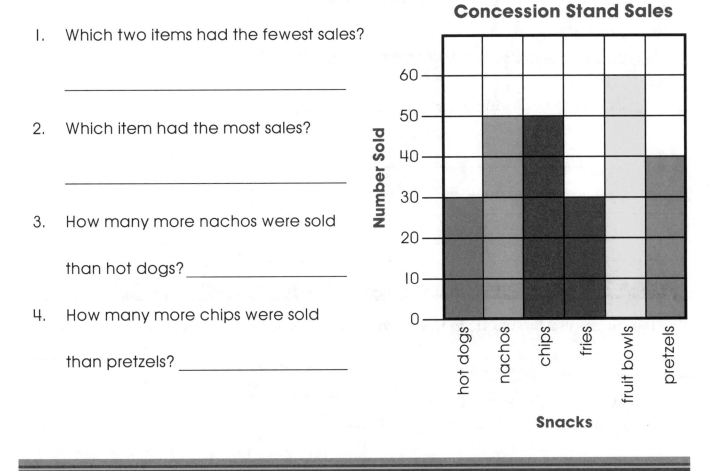

Concession Stand Sales

Number Sold

60
50
40
30
20
10
0

hot dogs   nachos   chips   fries   fruit bowls   pretzels

Snacks

Write three sentences. Use a word from the word bank in each sentence. Use capital letters, periods, question marks, and exclamation points where they are needed.

adult	during	finish	interested
job	prepare	summer	work

5. _____

6. _____

7. _____

DAY 18

Read the paragraph. Then, write the sounds that Nick heard.

Interesting Sounds

Nick heard the wind howling outside and the phone ringing inside. He heard his mother and father talking softly. His sister was singing to their baby brother. The baby was crying in his crib. The turtle in the tank was splashing in the water. The dog was barking at a cat. Nick could hear a lot of interesting things.

_____

_____

_____

Use the clues and the words in the word bank to complete the crossword puzzle.

camera	agree
rake	milk
cheese	microphone

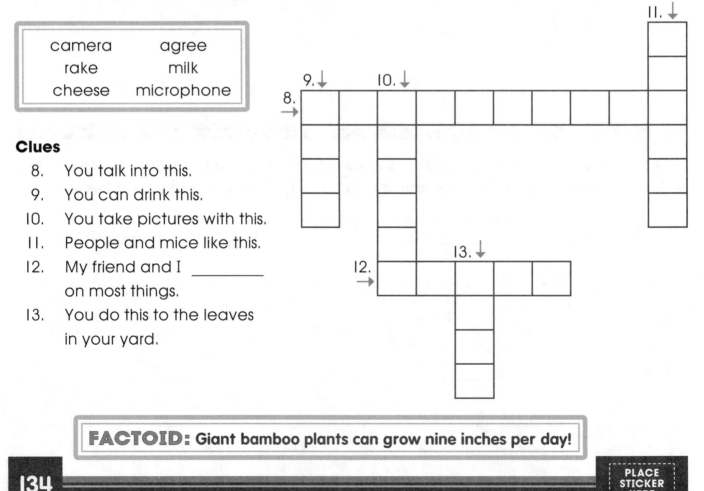

Clues

8.   You talk into this.
9.   You can drink this.
10. You take pictures with this.
11. People and mice like this.
12. My friend and I _____ on most things.
13. You do this to the leaves in your yard.

FACTOID: Giant bamboo plants can grow nine inches per day!

PLACE STICKER HERE

The line graph shows precipitation changes during a year in Chicago, Illinois. Use the line graph to answer the questions.

Precipitation Changes

1. Which three months received the same amount of rain?

   _____

2. What was the most rainfall received in one month? _____

3. Which month received the least amount of precipitation?_____

Write the word *Who*, *What*, *When*, *Why*, or *Where* to complete each sentence.

4. _____ will it be time to leave?

5. _____ wants to go to the park with me?

6. _____ didn't you do your work?

7. _____ should we go after the movie?

8. _____ time is it?

DAY 19

Read the story. Number the events in the order that they happened.

The Alarm Clock

Patrick was sleeping when his alarm clock started ringing. He jumped up, made his bed, and washed his face. Patrick put on his clothes and started going downstairs to eat breakfast. When he passed the window in the hall, he saw that it was still night. "Oh, no," he said, "my alarm clock went off at the wrong time!" Patrick went back to his bedroom and got back into bed.

9. _____ Patrick went back to bed.

10. _____ Patrick's alarm clock rang.

11. _____ Patrick saw that it was still night.

12. _____ Patrick made his bed and washed his face.

13. _____ Patrick started going downstairs to eat breakfast.

What would you do if you woke up and you had become your mom or dad? What would your day be like?

_____

_____

_____

_____

_____

FITNESS FLASH: Hop on your right foot for 30 seconds.

* See page ii.

PLACE STICKER HERE

Study the pictograph. Then, answer the questions.

Number of Flowers Picked

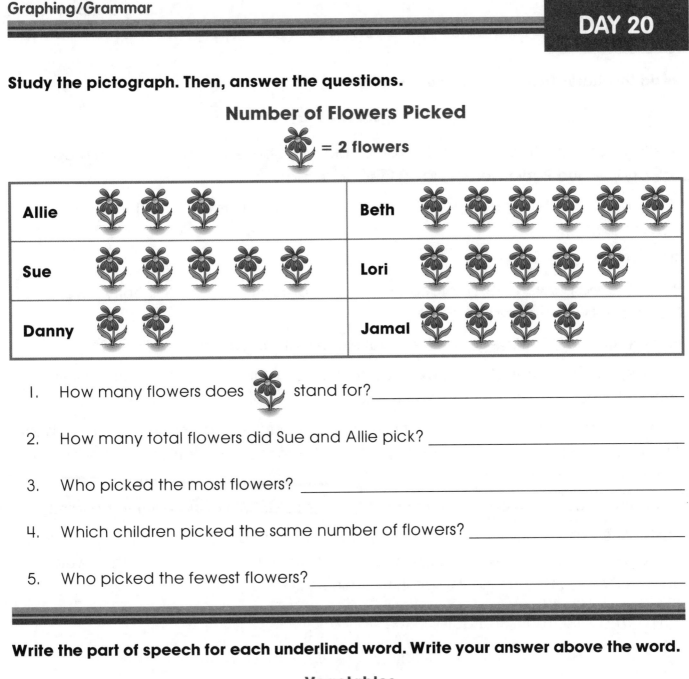

= 2 flowers

1. How many flowers does stand for? _____

2. How many total flowers did Sue and Allie pick? _____

3. Who picked the most flowers? _____

4. Which children picked the same number of flowers? _____

5. Who picked the fewest flowers? _____

Write the part of speech for each underlined word. Write your answer above the word.

Vegetables

Do you like <u>vegetables</u>? I like some vegetables. I do not like others. I like snow peas.

<u>They</u> taste best fresh from the garden. They are green and sweet. I like fresh, <u>crunchy</u>

carrots too. I pick them from the garden. I <u>love</u> corn on the cob. I pull off the husks.

Mom <u>boils</u> the corn. I eat the <u>yellow</u> corn from one end to the other.

DAY 20

Read the story. Then, answer the questions.

Ready for the Play-Off

Austin was too excited about the baseball play-off game to think about the model volcano he and Pablo were building in science class.

"Do you want to tear the paper into strips or dip them in paste and put them on?" Pablo asked.

"Home run!" said Austin.

Pablo looked puzzled. Austin's face burned with embarrassment. "I'm sorry. I was thinking about the game."

Pablo laughed. "Oh!" he said. "Well, that explains it. Do you think we'll win?"

"My big brother says that Ms. Lee's class hasn't won a play-off game in at least five years. Maybe we'll be the first," Austin said.

Austin saw Ms. Lee walking toward them. He picked up a piece of newspaper and tore it into strips. Pablo understood. He dipped a strip into the paste and smoothed it onto the side of the model volcano.

"You boys should start cleaning up now," Ms. Lee said. "We don't want to be late."

Austin and Pablo carried their model to the science table, put the lid on the paste container, recycled the extra newspaper, and cleaned their work area. They were back in their seats and ready to go in five minutes.

6. Who is the main character in the story?

    A. Austin's brother   B. Austin   C. Ms. Lee

7. What does the main character want to do? _____

    _____

8. Where does the story take place?

    A. in a classroom   B. in a gym   C. on the baseball field

> **CHARACTER CHECK:** Use a dictionary to look up the word *consequence*. Why should you think about consequences?

PLACE STICKER HERE

An Oily Separation

How can a mixture of oil and water be separated?

Materials:

- 16-ounce clear drinking glass
- spoon
- eyedropper
- 6.75 ounces (200 mL) of water
- 6.75 ounces (200 mL) of vegetable oil
- clear glass measuring cup

Procedure:

Pour the water into the drinking glass. Add the vegetable oil to the water. Stir the water and oil with the spoon and observe. Then, let the water and oil sit for 10–15 minutes.

Use the eyedropper to pull the oil from the top of the water and place it into the measuring cup. Record the amount of oil collected. Then, subtract that amount from the amount of oil that was first added to the drinking glass. Record your results. Then, try the experiment two more times. Record your data in the table.

Trial	Initial Volume of Oil	Volume of Oil Collected	Final Volume of Oil
1			
2			
3			

1. What happens when you stir the water and the oil? _____

    _____

2. What happens when you stop stirring the water and the oil? _____

    _____

What's This All About?

Sometimes, liquids separate into layers. Oil and water separate into layers. Water is heavier than oil, so it sinks to the bottom of a container.

BONUS

Disappearing Act

Water can disappear by evaporating. Sometimes, water leaves things behind when it evaporates.

Materials:

- masking tape
- 2 pie tins
- drinking glass
- 1 tablespoon of salt
- measuring cup
- pencil
- water
- spoon

Procedure:

Use the masking tape and a pencil to label the outside of the pie tins. Label the first pie tin *salt water* and the second pie tin *tap water*.

Use the measuring cup to pour 4 ounces (11.8 cL) of warm water into a drinking glass. Add one tablespoon of salt to the water. Use the spoon to stir the water until the salt dissolves. Add salt until no more will dissolve. This is called a saturated solution. Pour the saturated solution into the pie tin labeled *salt water*.

Use the measuring cup to pour 4 ounces (11.8 cL) of tap water into the pie tin labeled *tap water*. Put the pie tins side-by-side in a safe place. Record your observations each day until the water in both pie tins has evaporated.

What's This All About?

This activity uses salt water as the basis for crystal formation. The water evaporates from the pan. Salt, a mineral, stays in the pan.

More Fun Ideas to Try:

- Change the amount of salt in the water. Find out if it affects how quickly the water evaporates.
- With an adult, change the liquid you use. Try vinegar, lemonade, etc. Use the same amount of salt and change the amount of liquid.

Land Features

Look at the map. Write the letter of each landform next to its name.

1. _____ lake

2. _____ valley

3. _____ river

4. _____ peninsula

5. _____ volcano

6. _____ island

7. _____ mountain

8. _____ ocean

9. _____ savanna

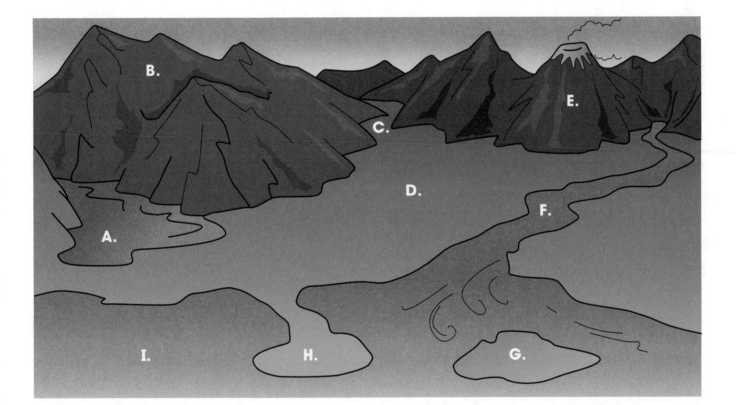

BONUS

Countries and Cities

Political maps show landmasses divided into regions such as countries and cities. Study a map of North America in an atlas or on the Internet. Then, draw a line to connect each city to its country. You will use each country more than once.

City

1. Mexico City
2. Toronto
3. Washington, D.C.
4. Montreal
5. Chicago
6. Acapulco
7. Boston
8. Guadalajara
9. Phoenix
10. New York City

Country

Mexico

Canada

United States of America

Choose one country from the list above, or pick a country you are interested in studying. Use an encyclopedia or the Internet to find information about this country. Then, write three facts about the country on the lines.

_____

_____

_____

_____

_____

_____

Democratic Governments

Read the passage. Then, answer the questions.

There are many types of government. One type of government is a democratic government. A democratic government gives its citizens the power to make decisions.

The United States has a democratic government. In the United States, citizens elect a president. The president is the head of the government. The citizens also elect people to Congress. Congress is the branch of government that makes laws. Great Britain also has a democratic government. The prime minister is the head of the government in Great Britain. The prime minister also helps make laws.

1. There are many types of _____ .

2. A _____ government gives its citizens the power to make decisions.

3. In the United States, the _____ elect a president.

4. In the United States, the _____ is the head of the government.

5. Citizens of the United States also elect people to _____ .

6. Congress is the branch of government that makes _____ .

7. In Great Britain, the _____ helps make the laws.

BONUS

Take It Outside!

Summer is full of spectacular scenes and inspiration. One of the most amazing sights of summer is the bright and beautiful flowers. Look for an interesting plant that catches your attention or a pretty flower in a garden or field. Instead of picking the plant or flower, keep it alive and pass on its beauty to others. Take a photograph of your plant or draw a picture of it. Turn your flower artwork into a "thinking of you" card and send it to someone you are not able to see this summer.

Math is everywhere—even outside! Watch for word problem opportunities when you are outdoors. For example, if you see 12 seagulls flying in the air, 3 more splashing in a puddle, and 16 sitting on the pier, write these facts on a piece of paper and turn them into a word problem. Solve the problem. Then, challenge your family and friends with your outdoor math problem.

With an adult, find a few different flowers outside. Look at each flower and identify its parts (petal, sepal, carpel, stamen, and stigma). Compare each flower's parts with the others parts' to find the similarities and differences.

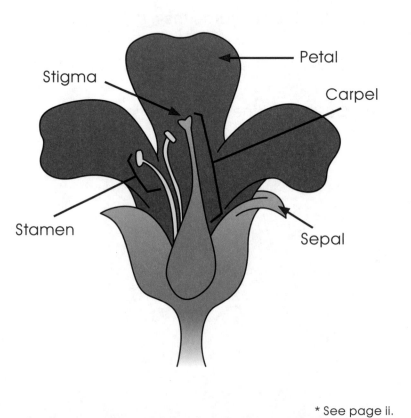

* See page ii.

Section I

Day 1: 1. 45; 2. 58; 3. 81; 4. 30; 5. 3; 6. 15; From left to right and top to bottom: zero, twenty, thirty, forty, sixty, eighty; Students should write the following words under *person*: aunt, officer, prince, friend; Students should write the following words under *place*: city, gym, store, desert; Students should write the following words under *thing*: cloud, letter, plate, shoe; 7. 1, 1; 8. 1, 1; 9. 2, 2; 10. 3, 3; 11. 2, 2; 12. 2, 2; 13. 3, 3; 14. 1, 1; 15. 1, 1; Students should write the following words under the celery: cell, century, cent, city; Students should write the following words under the carrot: cake, cat, cave, coat.

Day 2: 1. twenty, twentieth; 2. 60, sixtieth; 3. 36, thirty-sixth; 4. seventy-seven, seventy-seventh; 5. 5, five; 6. boy, shell, beach; 7. aunt, store, country; 8. cloud, rabbit; 9. letter, friend; 10. girl, glass, kitchen; 11. kite, breeze; 12. Anna, book, manatees; 13. Owen, Caron, cave; 14. pencil, sundae, helmet, dragon; 15. blossom, rabbit, spider, tiger; 16. carrot, puppy, candy, seven; 17. wonder, summer, cricket, marry; 18. candle, pencil, muffin, circus; 19. peanut, dollar, mitten, window

Day 3: 1. 346; 2. 527; 3. 831; 4. 730; 5. 292; 6. 214; 7. 428; 8. 400; 9. 479; 10. 872; 11. 680; 12. 722; 13. 399; 14. 600; 15. 735; 16. person; 17. place; 18. person; 19. thing; 20. thing; 21. place, 22. person; 23. thing; 24. C; 25. honey; 26. They move pollen from flower to flower;

27. They eat insects that chew on plants; 28. flies, crickets, and moths

Day 4: 1. <; 2. >; 3. >; 4. <; 5. <; 6. >; 7. >; 8. <; 9. <; 10. <; 11. >; 12. <; 13. mud; 14. camera; 15. bike; 16. bank; 17. hero; 18. palace; 19. run; 20. trail; 21. woods; 22. notice; 23. outdoors; 24. happy; 25. L; 26. S; 27. L; 28. S; 29. S; 30. L; 31. S; 32. L; 33. L; 34. S; 35. L

Day 5: 1. 2 tens; 2. 1 ten; 3. 3 ones; 4. 3 tens; 5. 0 ones; 6. 4 ones; 7. 7 tens; 8. 9 ones; 9. Cindy Lewis; 10. Nicholas Jones; 11. Ms. Cohen; 12. Don Li; 13. Mr. Finley; 14. Ellen Garza; 15. Dr. Monica Seth; 16. bad; 17. dirty; 18. noisy; 19. sold; 20. old; 21. short; 22. long; 23. short; 24. short; 25. long; 26. short; 27. long; 28. short; 29. short; 30. long; 31. short; 32. long; 33. long; 34. short; 35. long; 36. long

Day 6: 1. 629, 682, 636, 660; 2. 79, 429, 609, 509, 889, 69, 209; 3. 231, 38, 1,639, 530, 333, 32; 4. 54, 151, 555, 250, 58, 50, 255; 5. 1,423, 484, 432, 4,422; 6. 27, 147, 607, 447, 997, 1,007; 7. Jefferson Library; 8. Woodland School; 9. France; 10. Roberto's; 11. Fifi; 12. Julia; 13. Renee; 14. A; 15. travel quickly and easily from one coast of the United States to the other; 16. eastern and western parts of the country; 17. a golden nail

Day 7:

1. (7)816   121   (6)211
   44   729   (4)864

2. 26(84(2)   463(
   924(19(84(6)

3. (4)81   (6)43   (9)70
   1,294   1,122   2,361

4. 6 ones; 5. 2 hundreds; Students should write the following words under *noun*: farmer, man, park, teacher, ticket; Students should write the following words under *proper noun*: April, Mexico City, Ms. Sho, Sunny Market, Thursday; 6. right; 7. one; 8. wood; 9. bee; 10. new

Day 8: 1. 9; 2. 3; 3. 11; 4. 8; 5. 9; 6. 1; 7. 5; 8. 3; 9. 8; 10. 4; 11. 2; 12. 10; 13. 5; 14. 4; 15. 4; Students should write the following words under *singular*: fork, guitar, peanut, pond; Students should write the following words under *plural*: crickets, keys, shirts, toes; 16. re-, D; 17. un-, B; 18. mis-, A; 19. un-, E; 20. *mis*-, C; 21. 2, 2; 22. 4, 2; 23. 1, 1; 24. 3, 3; 25. 2, 1; 26. 1, 1; 27. 2, 2; 28. 2, 2; 29. 3, 3; 30. 2, 2; 31. 2, 1; 32. 2, 2; 33. 2, 1; 34. 3, 2; 35. 5, 3; 36. 2, 2

Day 9: 1. 6 + 5 = 11, 5 + 6 = 11, 11 − 6 = 5, 11 − 5 = 6; 2. 4 + 5 = 9, 5 + 4 = 9, 9 − 5 = 4, 9 − 4 = 5; 3. 7 + 5 = 12, 5 + 7 = 12, 12 − 7 = 5, 12 − 5 = 7; 4. tree; 5. apples; 6. treat; 7. flags; 8. swings; 9. sister; 10. pictures; 11. -ness; 12. -less; 13. -ness; 14. -ness; 15. -ness; Students should write the following words under the fly: dry, eye, sky; Students should write the following words under the baby: city, happy, story.

Day 10: 1. +; 2. −; 3. −; 4. =; 5. +; 6. −; 7. −; 8. −; 9. =; 10. −; 11. =; 12. +; 13. +; 14. +; 15. −; 16. girls; 17. dish; 18. pencil; 19. books; 20. inches; 21. boats; 22. pie; 23. shoes; 24. paper; 25. gift; 26. rain/drop; 27. light/house; 28. door/bell; 29. barn/yard; 30. bed/room; 31. snow/flakes

Day 11: 1. 6 baseballs; 2. 2 apples; 3. 5 miles; 4. 12 puppies; 5. book, books; 6. peach, peaches; 7. nest, nests; 8. A, B; 9. B, A; 10. B, A; Students should circle the following words: zoo, hoop, soon, pool, scoop, cool, stool, food, moon, moose, goose, school, tool, boot, spoon; Students should draw Xs on the following words: book, wool, cook, hood, took, foot, wood, crook.

Day 12: 1. A; 2. I; 3. B; 4. D; 5. E; 6. J; 7. K; 8. F; 9. G; 10. H; 11. men; 12. teeth; 13. leaves; 14. geese; 15. knives; 16. mice; 17. feet; Students should write the following words under *animals*: fox, elephant, bear, deer; Students should write the following words under *tools*: saw, pliers, hammer, screwdriver; Students should write the following words under *clothing*: shirt, pants, socks, hat; 18. street; 19. through; 20. sprang; 21. splash or thrash; 22. split; 23. throw; 24. strong or throng; 25. spree or three; 26. spray or stray; 27. splatter

Day 13: 1. 7; 2. 10; 3. 7; 4. 10; 5. 10; 6. 9; 7. 12; 8. 14; 9. 11; 10. 11; 11. 6; 12. 8; 13. 9; 14. 7; 15. 10;

16. 13; 17. It; 18. They; 19. He; 20. She; 21. C; 22. as long as it takes to sing the alphabet; 23. washes away germs that make you sick; 24. B; 25. You could pass the sickness to a friend and spread the germs to your eyes and mouth.

Day 14: 1. 9; 2. 7; 3. 9; 4. 8; 5. 7; 6. 8; 7. 8; 8. 7; 9. 9; 10. 8; 11. horses; 12. aunt; 13. bike; 14. umbrella; 15. I planted seeds; 16. Luke started his car; 17. I put on my socks; 18. We built a snowman; 19. I put toothpaste on my toothbrush; 20. I climbed into bed.

Day 15: 1. =, <, >; 2. <, =, =; 3. =, <, <; 4. =, <, =; 5. >, <, =; 6. fruit; 7. José and Henry; 8. family and I; 9. Marisa; 10. flowers; 11. Daniel; 12. C

Day 16: 1. 4 flowers; 2. 4 miles; 3. 4 cars; 4. 18 toys; 5. listens; 6. works; 7. rides; 8. spills; 9. finds; 10. A; 11. oceans, lakes, and streams; 12. drops of water rise into the air; 13. when the air cools; 14. They produce rain, snow, sleet, or hail; 15. soil, oceans, lakes, and streams

Day 17: 1. 42; 2. 24; 3. 89; 4. 14; 5. 78; 6. 12; 7. 13; 8. 0; 9. 35; 10. 48; 11. 86; 12. 97; 13. 6; 14. 14; 15. 11; 16. runs; 17. thinks; 18. goes; 19. paints; 20. climb; 21. builds; 22. go; 23. float; 24. watches; 25. eats; 26. B; 27. A; 28. phone; 29. elephants; 30. alphabet; 31. amphibian

Day 18: 1. 449; 2. 977; 3. 889; 4. 338; 5. 199; 6. 757; 7. 748; 8. 747; 9. 592; 10. 288; 11. 907; 12. 895; 13. 609; 14. 800; 15. 978; 16. -ed; 17. -d; 18. -ed; 19. -ed; 20. -ed;

21. -ed; 22. -d; 23. -d; 24. -d; 25. -ed; 26. -ed; 27. -d; 28. -ed; 29. -d; 30. J. T., David's; 31. Kendra, Evan; 32. Squeeze; 33. quilt; 34. quiet; 35. quarter; 36. queen; 37. question

Day 19: 1. 632; 2. 100; 3. 643; 4. 813; 5. 175; 6. 562; 7. 422; 8. 817; 9. 72; 10. 56; 11. 431; 12. 245; 13. 831; 14. 500; 15. 757; 16. picked; 17. smiled; 18. searched; 19. rode; 20. asked; 21. mended; 22. mixed; 23. jump into bed too; 24. the boy; 25. everywhere the boy goes; 26. Answers will vary but may include: during the day, when a light is on, etc.; 27. w; 28. b; 29. k; 30. k; 31. k, gh; 32. b

Day 20: 1. 441; 2. 855; 3. 363; 4. 413; 5. 106; 6. 59; 7. 276; 8. 203; 9. 568; 10. 778; 11. 993; 12. 786; 13. 999; 14. 900; 15. 797; Students should write the following words under *present*: blow, find, fly, know, laugh, wear; Students should write the following words under *past*: blew, flew, found, knew, laughed, wore; 16. F; 17. R; 18. R; 19. F; 20. F; 21. R; 22. F; 23. R; 24. F; 25. F

Fluid Motion: 1. the marble that traveled through water; 2. Answers will vary.

X Marks the Spot: Yellow Sands

What's the Key?:

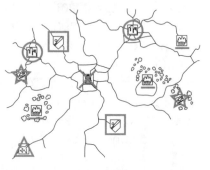

Brent's Street Map: I. Shady Oaks Street; 2. Clear Creek Road; 3. Main Street; 4. Windy Way; 5. Walnut Street; 6. Shady Oaks Street and Park Street

Section II

Day I: I. 55; 2. 27; 3. 64; 4. 31; 5. 72; 6. 80; 7. 52; 8. 42; 9. 33; 10. 20; 11. 41; 12. 54; 13. 28; 14. 35; 15. E; 16. A; 17. F; 18. G; 19. C; 20. B; 21. D; 22. 3, 2, 2; 23. 3, 3, 3; 24. 2, 2, 2; 25. 2, 2, 2; 26. 2, 1, 1; 27. 3, 3, 3; 28. 2, 2, 2; 29. incorrect; 30. incorrect; 31. correct; 32. incorrect; 33. correct

Day 2: I. 49; 2. 45; 3. 8; 4. 56; 5. 59; 6. 17; 7. 39; 8. 75; 9. 15; 10. 46; 11. 19; 12. made; 13. took; 14. bought; 15. saw; 16. went; 17. flew; 18. A; 19. C; 20. play outside, go swimming

Day 3: I. 51; 2. 34; 3. 39; 4. 48; 5. 82; 6. 26; 7. 25; 8. 81; 9. 28; 10. 92; 11. 10; 12. 42; 13. 40; 14. 15; 15. 81; 16. am; 17. is; 18. are; 19. am; 20. are; 21. is; 22. are; 23. leaped; 24. yell; 25. giggling; 26. largest; 27. creek; 28. middle

Day 4: I. 46; 2. 181; 3. 84; 4. 178; 5. 183; 6. 50; 7. 127; 8. 97; 9. 124; 10. am; 11. are; 12. am; 13. is; 14. are; 15. am; 16. is; 17. is; 18. are; 19. antonyms; 20. synonyms; 21. homophones; 22. synonyms; 23. antonyms; 24. homophones; 25. antonyms; gas, solid, liquid, Matter, solid, liquid, gas

Day 5: I. √; 2. X; 3. √; 4. X; 5. √; 6. X; 7. X; 8. √; 9. X; 10. √; 11. √; 12. √; 13. X; 14. √; 15. X; 16. have; 17. has; 18. has; 19. has; 20. have; 21. have; 22. has; 23. has; 24. B; 25. F; 26. T; 27. T; 28. F

Day 6: I. 1:25; 2. 11:05; 3. 3:55; 4. 2:35; 5. 10:40; 6. 7:20; 7. going; 8. saying; 9. doing; 10. sleeping; 11. walking; 12. reading; 13. painting; 14. working; 15. eating; 16. spelling; 17. cooking; 18. watching; 19. unsure, not sure; 20. unhappy, not happy; 21. unlike, not like; 22. rewrite, write again; 23. retell, tell again; 24. reprint, print again

Day 7:

7. raked, raking; 8. jumped, jumping; 9. hugged, hugging; 10. cooked, cooking; 11. skated, skating; 12. wrapped, wrapping; 13. sneezed, sneezing; 14. popped, popping; 15. talked, talking; 16. smiled, smiling; 17. C; 18. E; 19. D; 20. B; 21. A; 22. D; 23. C

Day 8:

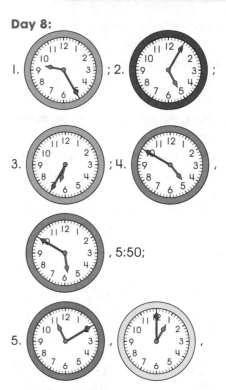

, 5:50;

12:10; 6. went; 7. gone; 8. went; 9. gone; 10. went; 11. more than 900; 12. insects, fruit, and nectar; 13. 16 inches (40 cm) in length; 14. Bats eat insects, pollinate plants, and spread seeds; 15. mosquitoes, mayflies, and moths

Day 9:

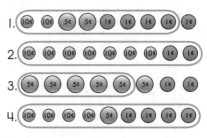

5. stop, stopping, stopped; 6. clap, clapping, clapped; 7. hopping, hopped, hop; 8. classmates; 9. barefoot; 10. springtime; 11. dinnertime; 12. seashells

Day 10: I. 88¢; 2. 77¢; 3. 62¢; 4. 51¢; 5. 75¢; Yesterday, we **learned** about colors in art. We made a color wheel. We found out that there **are** three basic colors. They **are** called primary colors. Red, yellow, and blue are primary colors. Primary colors mix to make other colors. Red and yellow **make** orange. Yellow and blue make green. Blue and red make purple. Orange, green, and purple **are** secondary colors; 6. B; 7. A; 8. B; 9. A; 10. A; 11. beak; 12. eye; 13. feet; 14. tail; 15. wing

Day 11:

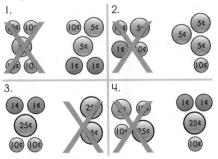

5. equal; 6. tiny; 7. low; 8. rainy; 9. B; 10. Africa, Antarctica, Asia, Australia, Europe, North America, South America; 11. millions of years ago; 12. jungle; 13. They were once one piece of land.

Day 12: 1–5. Answers will vary; 6. soft; 7. steep; 8. screechy; 9. hot, wet; Students should follow the directions.

Day 13: 1. 46; 2. 7; 3. 19; 4. 72; 5. 39; 6. 72; 7. 93; 8. 7; 9. 19; 10. 64; 11. 59; 12. 95; 13. 8; 14. 92; 15. 47; 16. 83; 17. 55; 18. 45; 19. blue, purple; 20. little, green; 21. colorful, soft; 22. dark, gray; 23. new, brown; 24. 2; 25. 1; 26. 4; 27. 3

Day 14: 1. 1 + 3 + 1 = 5 inches; 2. 3 + 2 + 1 = 6 inches; 3. 1 + 4 + 2 = 7 inches; 4. faster, fastest; 5. taller, tallest; 6. colder, coldest; 7. A; 8. 8–11 hours each night;

9. You might have trouble paying attention to your teacher; 10. read a book; 11. C

Day 15: 1. 7 cm; 2. 8 cm; 3. 9 cm; 4. 3 cm; 5. 5 cm; 6. 4 cm; 7–11. Answers will vary; 12. C; 13. B; 14–21. Answers will vary.

Day 16: 1. A; 2. B; 3. A; 4. B; 5. B; 6. I am; 7. you will; 8. would not; 9. we have; 10. we would; 11. you are; 12. she is; 13. is not; 14. I will; 15. page 4; 16. Chapter 3; 17. page 26; 18. All About Ants; 19. electric; 20. train; 21. keep; 22. truck; 23. play

Day 17: 1. Students should circle the tablespoon; 2. Students should circle the gallon; 3. Students should circle the 1 cup measure; 4. she is; 5. he is; 6. are not; 7. you have; 8. I have; 9. I would; 10. it is; 11. have not; 12. she will; 13. should not; 14. we will; 15. we are; 16. C; 17. B; 18. A; 19. B

Day 18: 1. 10, cold; 2. 90, warm; 3. 20, cold; 4. 70, warm; 5. We'll; 6. I'll; 7. We've; 8. We're; 9. B; 10. M; 11. B; 12. J; 13. M; 14. J; 15. B; 16. B; 17. J; 18. B; 19. E; 20. A; 21. D; 22. F; 23. C; 24. B

Day 19: 1. Monday, Friday, Sunday; 2. Saturday; 3. Saturday, Thursday; 4. Tuesday, Wednesday; 5. December—Dec., Doctor—Dr., Thursday—Thurs., ounce—oz., January—Jan.; 6. Mister—Mr., October—Oct., foot—ft., Avenue—Ave., Road—Rd.; 7. yard—yd., March—Mar., Junior—Jr., inch—in., Wednesday—Wed.; 8. Saturday—Sat., Senior—Sr., Monday—Mon., Fahrenheit—F, Street—St.; 9. are; 10. bird; 11. bud; 12. card; 13. dark;

14. first; 15. her; 16. more; 17. part; 18. third; 19. turn; 20. word

Day 20: 1. triangle; 2. square; 3. hexagon; 4. circle; 5. rhombus; 6. rectangle; 7. octagon; 8. pentagon; 9. yes; 10. yes; 11. no; 12. no; 13. no; 14. no; 15. yes; 16. A; 17.

Alike or Different?	Grass	Tree
living thing	X	X
stands straight in the wind		X
bends in the wind	X	
tall		X
small	X	
can be climbed		X
can be sat on	X	
green in color	X	X

Locate It!: 1. H,1; 2. G,5; 3. B,6; 4. E,1; 5. D,4; 6. A,4; 7. E,5

Silver City Championship:

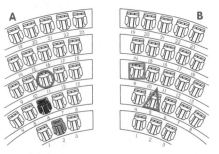

Continent Scramble: 1. C, Africa; 2. A, North America; 3. D, Europe; 4. B, South America; 5. E, Asia; 6. G, Antarctica; 7. F, Australia

Section III

Day 1: 1. Students should circle the square; 2. Students should circle the square; 3. Students should circle the circle; 4. Students should circle the circle; 5. The ice is in the glass; 6. Put the plant on the porch; 7. The lamp is on the desk; 8. Please answer the phone; 9. I will walk the dog; 10. Rain is good for the lawn; 11. Did you see my keys; 12. Hugo plays the piano;

13. B; 14. C; Students should write the following words under *animals*: fox, horse, monkey, tiger; Students should write the following words under *toys*: ball, blocks, doll, kite; Students should write the following words under *food*: beans, bread, cheese, corn.

Day 2: 1. 6; 2. 2, 3; 3. 1, 4; 4. 2, 4; 5. D; 6. D; 7. ND; 8. ND; 9. D; 10. ND; 11. D; 12. D; 13. I left my notebook there.; 14. Anna ate four grapes.; 15. Isabelle smelled the wildflowers.; 16. I like snapping turtles.; 17. Do donkeys eat hay?; 18. Be careful in the water.

Day 3: 1. 36; 2. 57; 3. 57; 4. 88; 5. 69; 6. 64; 7. 63; 8. 34; 9. 25; 10. 22; 11. 71; 12. 83; 13. 81; 14. 64; 15. 73; 16. I; 17. D; 18. D; 19. I; 20. I; 21. I; 22. D; 23. D; 24. A; 25. C; 26. A

Day 4: 1. A; 2. D; 3. C; 4. Answers will vary; 5. Is the man Gary's father?; 6. Can she ride her new bike?; 7. Will I ride the black horse?; 8. paw; 9. math; 10. bison; 11. hand; 12. race

Day 5:

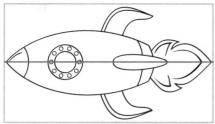

1. I; 2. E; 3. E; 4. E; 5. D; 6. I; 7. Watch out!; 8. I had a great day!; From left to right: pink, purple, white, orange, yellow; 9. Answers will vary but may include: act, arch, art, at, car, cart, cat, chat, hat, rat, tar,; 10. Answers will vary but may include: art, as, at, rat, sat, star, stat, tar, tart;

11. Answers will vary but may include: act, at, art, car, cart, cat, fact, fat, raft, rat, tar.

Day 6:

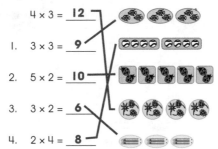

1. 3 × 3 = 9
2. 5 × 2 = 10
3. 3 × 2 = 6
4. 2 × 4 = 8
4 × 3 = 12

5. IM; 6. IM; 7. E; 8. IM; 9. IM; 10. D; 11. I; 12. E; 13. A; 14. 3, 1, 2, 4

Day 7: 1. 5; 2. 25; 3. 12; 4. 0; 5. 4; 6. 20; 7. 15; 8. 1; 9. 10; 10. 7; 11. 8; 12. 6; 13. 9; 14. 0; 15–18. Answers will vary; 19. noun; 20. 2. a bud or a seed; 21. after; 22. Answers will vary; 23. birds; 24. school supplies; 25. animals; 26. drinks

Day 8: 1. 3 × 4 = 12 flowers; 2. 4 × 5 = 20 pieces; 3. 3 × 2 = 6 straws; 4. 4 × 4 = 16 chairs; 5. .; 6. ?; 7. !; 8. ?; 9. .; 10. ?; 11. !; 12. She got up late today; 13. She missed the bus; 14. Answers will vary.

Day 9:

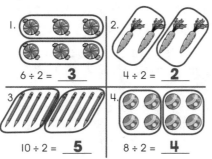

1. 6 ÷ 2 = 3
2. 4 ÷ 2 = 2
3. 10 ÷ 2 = 5
4. 8 ÷ 2 = 4

5. .; 6. ?; 7. !; 8. .; 9. .; 10. !; 11. ?; 12. *Lauren is very busy in the summer*; 13. eight o'clock; 14. She helps him work in the garden; 15. Answers will vary but may include: swimming, playing soccer, reading, playing with friends, and

riding her bike; 16. table; 17. clock; 18. donkey

Day 10:

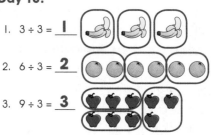

1. 3 ÷ 3 = 1
2. 6 ÷ 3 = 2
3. 9 ÷ 3 = 3

4. My Ride on a Donkey; 5. The Day I Missed School; 6. Fun, Fabulous Pets; 7. A Fire Drill; 8. My Summer Job; 9. yes; 10. part of speech (adjective); 11. Answers will vary; 12. clothes; 13. light; 14. rain

Day 11: 1. 6; 2. 6; 3. 7; 4. 9; 5. 7; 6. 7; 7. 9; 8. 9; 9. 7; 10. 9; 11. 9; 12. 7; **Mom, Dad,** and I went camping last week. We went with Uncle **Seth** and Aunt **Kay**. We had fun. Dad and **Uncle Seth** climbed on rocks. Aunt **Kay** and I saw a chipmunk. We hiked on exciting trails. There was only one problem. **Mom, Dad,** and I did not bring sweaters. Dad said that it would be warm in the desert. He was wrong. At night, it was very cold. **Uncle** Seth and **Aunt Kay** had sweaters. Mom, **Dad,** and I stayed close to the fire. Next time, we will bring warmer clothes; 13. reality; 14. fantasy; 15. reality; 16. fantasy; 17. flower; 18. bud; 19. root; 20. seed; 21. leaf; 22. stem

Day 12: 1. 5, 6, 7, 8, 9, 10, Rule: +1; 2. 12, 10, 8, 6, 4, 2, Rule: −2; 3. 50, 60, 70, 80, 90, 100, Rule: +10; 4. 25, 30, 35, 40, 45, 50, Rule: +5; 5. 18, 15, 12, 9, 6, 3, Rule: −3; 6. Dallas, Texas, .; 7. Mr. Javaris, .; 8. Is, Caleb's, April, ?; 9. My, i, Smith's,

Market, .; 10. What, ?;
11. B; 12. the Iowa State Fair; 13. It was bright yellow; 14. She was the first woman to fly alone across the Atlantic Ocean.; 15. She decided to fly around the world. Her plane was lost over the Pacific Ocean.

Day 13: 1. 6; 2. 3; 3. 8; 4. 7; 5. Where do birds live?; 6. My sister works very hard.; 7. She can swim like a fish./Can she swim like a fish?; 8. Why is grass green?; 9. Fish live in water.; 10. When can we go to the park?; 11. Why did she go to the store?; 12. What is his name?; 13. I love to play basketball.; 14. B

Day 14: 1. $\frac{1}{4}$; 2. $\frac{1}{3}$; 3. $\frac{1}{4}$; 4. $\frac{1}{3}$; 5. $\frac{1}{2}$; 6. $\frac{1}{5}$; 7. A.; 8. B.; 9. 26; 10. 31; 11. 15; 12. 21; 13. 60; 14. 42; 15–24. Answers will vary.

Day 15:

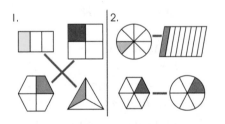

3. A.; 4. A.; 5. C; 6. all citizens over the age of 18; 7. 1920; 8. Adults of all races were given the right to vote; 9. People can help decide who serves in the government and what kinds of laws are passed.

Day 16:

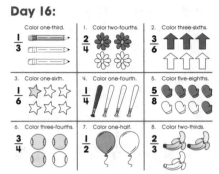

The earth has many mountains, rivers, lakes, oceans, and continents. The Andes, the Rockies, and the Urals are mountain ranges. The Amazon, the Nile, and the Hudson are rivers. Lake Erie, Lake Ontario, and Lake Huron are three of the Great Lakes. The Pacific, the Atlantic, and the Arctic are oceans. Europe, Asia, and Africa are continents. New Zealand, Greenland, and Iceland are islands. 9. Travis; 10. Keisha; 11. Lamar; 12. Mrs. Travers; 13. Sadaf; 14. Friday; 15. 5; 16. 26; 17. Friday

Day 17: 1. blue; 2. yellow; 3. green; 4. green; 5. Bobby has a dog named Shadow.; 6. Do bluebirds eat insects?; 7. Can I borrow your video game?; 8. My name is Nikki.; 9. ground; 10. trees; 11. window; 12. cow; 13. cat

Day 18: 1. hot dogs and fries; 2. fruit bowls; 3. 20; 4. 10; 5.–7. Answers will vary; howling, ringing, talking, singing, crying, splashing, barking;

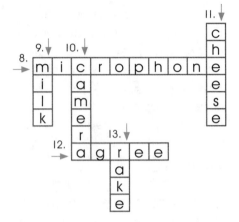

Day 19: 1. April, June, July; 2. 4.5 inches; 3. February; 4. When; 5. Who; 6. Why; 7. Where; 8. What; 9. 5; 10. 1; 11. 4; 12. 2; 13. 3

Day 20: 1. 2; 2. 16; 3. Beth; 4. Sue and Lori; 5. Danny; noun; pronoun; adjective; verb; verb; adjective; 6. B; 7. win the play-off game; 8. A

An Oily Separation: 1. It looks like they mix together; 2. They separate.

Land Features: 1. A; 2. C; 3. F; 4. H; 5. E; 6. G; 7. B; 8. I; 9. D

Countries and Cities: 1. Mexico; 2. Canada; 3. United States of America; 4. Canada; 5. United States of America; 6. Mexico; 7. United States of America; 8. Mexico; 9. United States of America; 10. United States of America

Types of Government:
1. government; 2. democratic; 3. citizens; 4. president; 5. Congress; 6. laws; 7. prime minister

The Original
Summer Bridge Activities™

Congratulations!

This certifies that

_____
Name

has completed **Summer Bridge Activities**™.

_____
Parent's Signature

www.carsondellosa.com